OPENING DAY

A Study of the
Book of Beginnings

By Dr. Elliot Johnson

OPENING DAY

ELLIOT JOHNSON

ISBN: 1-929478-60-7
SPRING TRAINING

ELLIOT JOHNSON

ISBN: 1-929478-44-5

CROSS TRAINING PUBLISHING
317 WEST SECOND STREET
GRAND ISLAND, NE 68801
(308) 384-5762

PUBLISHED BY CROSS TRAINING PUBLISHING,
317 WEST SECOND STREET
GRAND ISLAND, NE 68801

OPENING DAY

A Study of the
Book of Beginnings

By Dr. Elliot Johnson

CONTENTS

OPENING DAY

A Study of Genesis

Foreword

ALL HUMANS BRING PRESUPPOSITIONS and biases into their interpretations of books, events, and even other people. It seems fair to state mine.

I believe God's Word is an authoritative source of factual history. In fact, it's the only totally accurate history of mans' origin! Truth is revealed by an omniscient God and is never discovered by the rationalization of man. The facts of real science affirm Scripture. Therefore, the idea of evolution (all living things descended from organic molecules by random chance over millions of years through mutation, natural selection, and survival of the fittest) is science fiction. The sin of man brought about death and suffering. God created everything in six days and called it very good. He isn't to blame for the suffering in the world. We suffer and die because of the curse of sin. A worldwide flood vastly changed geologic processes so the earth can't be accurately dated by observation. God's Word, however, does give accurate genealogies, so we know earth's approximate age. Finally, we're accountable to our Creator. His name is Jesus Christ and one day we'll stand before Him to be judged.

Truth is unchanging and absolute. It's objective. Truth remains true no matter who believes it. Compromising the truth of Scripture never causes man to come to God.

Evolutionists believe truth is relative, changing, and to be discovered by the rationalism of natural man. They think as mans' ideas of truth change, truth changes. For example, it was ancient Greek "scientists" who came up with the idea that the earth was flat. Long before, Isaiah taught it was round (Isaiah 40:22). Later the scientists had to change their minds to agree with God's Word!

Evolutionists believe that changed governed by randomness continue at the same rates today as in the past.

Atheistic evolutionists believe there is no God. They credit natural processes for the development of life. The Bible calls these people fools (Psalms 14:1, 53:1). Theistic evolutionists believe God used millions of years of mutations, suffering, and death before Adam's sin to bring everything into existence. They deny the authority of Scripture, which destroys the very foundation of Christianity. The implications of their belief system are far-reaching.

Science is based upon observation and repeatability. The evidence observed by both creationists and evolutionists is the same. The biases of each determine their interpretation. These biases are matters of faith. The controversy isn't between science and faith. It's between faith in natural processes using random chance and faith in a sovereign, omnipotent God. No one is neutral. All are biased! An atheist can't even consider the question, "Did God create?" for to do so would mean he would cease his bias against God's existence and give up being an atheist! An agnostic believes he can't know anything for certain. He is 100 percent biased against absolute truth. He must reject any belief system that claims to know truth or he's no longer an agnostic. A creationist is also 100 percent biased, believing the God of history revealed truth in a book which claims over 3,000 times to be the Word of God. He can't consider the question, "Did God not create everything?" because the book starts with the assertion that God (the only one who was there at the time) created everything in six days and called it "very good!"

My bias is toward God and His Word. What's yours?

Dr. Elliot Johnson

OPENING DAY

A Study of Genesis

Introduction

OPENING DAY is a thrilling time for athletes in any sport. The preparations, expectations, and fresh start awaken excitement in every competitor. Enthusiasm is at its highest for teams on opening day!

"Opening day" at the creation of the universe was far more glorious than opening day at any ball park! All the "fans" (angels) shouted for joy (Job 38)! The scene is described in Genesis 1.

Genesis is the book of beginnings that prepares us for the end! The word "genesis" means "origin." In Genesis, we find the beginnings of time and space, earth, plants, animals, mankind, marriage, sin on earth, redemption, judgment, death, languages and nations. Genesis is the key to understanding God's plan. It covers a great number of years. There are at least 2,000 years from Genesis 1 (creation) to Genesis 11 (Abraham) and there are 2,000 years from Abraham to the birth of Jesus Christ.

Moses wrote Genesis probably around the time of the Exodus, in the 15th century B.C.. Because the Holy Spirit supernaturally inspired Moses, it may be said that Genesis gives the only true account of creation by the only one Who was there — the Creator Himself!

Genesis is the history book that is the foundation of all accurate history books. Since it begins at the beginning, nothing on earth has ever been "pre-historic." Only God existed in "prehistory!" The themes of blessing and cursing are woven throughout Genesis. Genesis 12-50 records the origin of God's "test tube" nation (Israel) through which He promised to bless the world. Israel is central to God's plan on earth. She was given the land of Canaan as a home forever. Her purpose was to reveal God and His nature to the world. Israel is a great object lesson, for her obedience to God always brought God's blessing and her disobedience always brought judgment.

May our worship of the Creator intensify, our understanding expand, and our obedience increase as we contemplate the opening day of God's creation and care for His creatures!

THE "BIG INNING"

In the beginning God created the heavens and the earth.
Genesis 1:1

EVERY COACH KNOWS it's vital to make a strong state-ment at the beginning of a game. We need to get started right. "Get ahead and stay ahead" is an oft-repeated motto.

God had no beginning, nor will He have an end. He always was and is! Scripture assumes His eternal exist-ence without trying to prove it. The Bible has a name ("fool)" for those who deny Him (Psalm 14:1, 53:1). The heavens, earth, animals, mankind, and all living things had a be-ginning. All were created ("bara" = "to create out of noth-ing)". Only God can create out of nothing. The creation magnifies Him as Sovereign Lord over all His creation.

How did God do it? Proverbs 3:19 says, "By wisdom the Lord laid the earth's foundations, by understanding He set the heavens in place; by His knowledge the deeps were divided and the clouds let drop the dew." The uni-verse was formed at God's command (Hebrews 11:3). He spoke it into existence (Psalm 33:9). God made the uni-verse through Jesus Christ (Hebrews 1:2). Colossians 1:16 says, "For by him all things were created; things in heaven and on earth, visible and invisible, whether thrones or powers or rulers or authorities; all things were created by him and for him." Verse 17 goes on to say that He holds everything together!

Certainly, God is a creative genius (Psalm 8:3, Psalm 104)! He provided light (Genesis 1:3), He is light (1 John 1:5), and in eternity future He will be the source of light (Revelation 21:23). Creation declares His glory (Psalm 19:1). He created everything for His pleasure (Revelation 4:11) and for His glory (Isaiah 43:7).

God used six days ("yom") to create everything. He de-fined "day" here as evening and morning (a 24-hour pe-riod). He rested on the seventh day to teach us something very special. We're to work for six days and rest for one day. The Sabbath became the sign of God's covenant with Israel and a picture of a believer's rest in Jesus (Hebrews 4). God called His creation "good" and "very good." Very likely, the earth was like a huge greenhouse covered by a canopy of water vapor. The temperature was uniform from pole to pole, high winds were nonexistent, a mist watered the earth, and the canopy filtered out ultraviolet rays which extended life into hundreds of years! It was evidently not until God destroyed life on earth in the Flood that the canopy collapsed and the ocean depths were "opened up." Psalm 18:15 reveals this great catastrophe of global proportions!

God's creation is orderly and self-perpetuating through His established laws. Animals were created "according to their kind" and God is through creating out of nothing (Hebrews 4:3). We still see much cooperation (symbiosis) in creation, in spite of competition. As Creator, He is Controller. He has the right to tell His creatures how to live. The One who controls the ocean boundaries (Job 38:8-11) also separates light from darkness, good from evil, blessing from cursing and holiness from sin. Nothing poses a threat to our Sovereign Creator!

ADAM AND THE TEST

And the Lord God commanded the man, "You are free to eat from any tree in the garden, but you must not eat from the tree of the knowledge of good and evil, for when you eat of it you will surely die."

Genesis 2:16-17

GAMES PROVIDE A TEST to contestants, just as exams provide an evaluation of students. The games measure physical ability, persistence, preparation, and discipline. Tests aren't bad things, though they can be challenging. They must be overcome!

Adam was given a test in Eden. He was given a free moral choice to obey God or to disobey. And God carefully explained the consequences of his choice! Let's look at the situation:

Hebrew literature often gives an overview followed by more detail. Accordingly, Genesis 2 further explains Day 6 of creation, when God formed Adam ("red" or "ground") from the dust of the earth. God breathed life into Adam, making him a spiritual being as well as a physical one. Unlike the animals, he was created in God's image. Man was created a spiritual being.

Life came directly from the hand and breath of God. God didn't "evolve" life over millions of years, but He formed man from earth in a single day and breathed life into his nostrils. Only science fiction, not real science, teaches evolution! We are the "work of His hand" (Isaiah 64:8). Elihu said, "The Spirit of God has made me; the breath of the Almighty gives me life" (Job 33:4).

God put Adam into a beautiful garden called Eden ("pleasantness") and gave him work to do. He had responsibility. He was not to be idle. God brought the animals to him and Adam named and remembered them all. God had given Adam the gift of language so he could communicate. Adam was an intellectual giant!

13

God placed two trees in the middle of His garden — the tree of life and the tree of the knowledge of good and evil (v 9). He placed only one restriction upon Adam. He wasn't to eat the fruit of the second tree. He was better off not to know evil, which he would only discover through disobedience. The man was given a choice of obedience or disobedience. It was a test of life or death. Death (spiritual separation from God followed by physical death) would result from failure to obey God. Was God trying to make man miserable? No! God wanted man to be perfectly happy and He knows we can only be happy in obedience to our Creator!

God created man with a purpose in mind. We were created to worship God. We are to kneel before Him (Psalm 95:6). He made us and we are the "sheep" of His pasture (Psalm 100:3). We were made for God's glory (Isaiah 43:7). We were made to make God's wisdom known (Ephesians 3:10-11).

What a wonderful creation! Man was serving God in a perfect environment. Everything was perfect. So far, so good!

EVE

The Lord God said, "It's not good for the man to be alone. I will make a helper suitable for him."

Genesis 2:18

GOOD COACHES CONSTANTLY stress improvement of their teams. As coach Chuck Knox once stated, "Practice without improvement is meaningless."

God had created everything perfect, so what He had created couldn't be improved upon! But just when it seemed the situation couldn't be any better for Adam, God made it better! The Lord said that being alone wasn't good. There was no suitable companion for Adam since he wasn't an animal, nor was he related to them. So He anesthetized Adam, removed a rib, and constructed a woman. The first surgery resulted in a new life! God invented marriage, as He created the woman and brought her to Adam to help him. The woman was formed from Adam's side to be near him and to be protected by him. Adam named the woman "Eve" ("living"), for she would become the mother of all living (3:20). It was the world's first and only perfect marriage, for it matched two perfect creatures.

God created the man and the woman to be a pair. His plan was one man for one woman for life. The birth rates of boys and girls are nearly equal and His plan has not changed. From this Scripture and others, it's clear that God's will for man was monogamy from the very beginning (Deuteronomy 17:17; Matthew 19:9; Ephesians 5:23-33).

In this perfect world, Adam and Eve wore no clothes. There was no sin, shame, or fear. The climate on earth was mild from pole to pole. Everything was still positive — so far!

DISASTER

When the woman saw that the fruit of the tree was good for food and pleasing to the eye and also desirable for gaining wisdom, she took some and ate it. She also gave some to her husband, who was with her, and he ate it.

Genesis 3:6

SOMETHING TERRIBLE HAPPENED to the Kentucky Wildcats in the spring of 2002. They held a seven-run lead over Pepperdine going into the bottom of the ninth inning. Did they win? No! The Waves rallied to score eight runs against four Kentucky pitchers and captured an 18-17 victory! It was a disaster for the Wildcats and coach Keith Madison.

Chapter 3 of Genesis is a "pivot point" in Scripture. Our understanding of life on earth depends upon this chapter. Something terrible happened here. In Chapters 1-2 everything is perfect, but beginning in Chapter 4, we see jealousy, anger, murder, lying, corruption, rebellion, and judgment. What has happened? It's called "sin."

A subtle serpent inhabited by a power more potent than Darth Vador of *Star Wars* or Voldemort ("lord full of death") of *Lord of the Rings* appears in Eden. We aren't told how he got to Eve, but he indwelt a beautiful upright creature who spoke to the woman. This dark, sinister power is named "Satan" and his origin seems to be recorded in Isaiah 14 and Ezekiel 28. He was formerly an angel in heaven, from which he fell shortly after creation (Job 38:7). Avoiding the man, he approached the woman and probably made small talk about the beauty of everything. Then he planted a suggestion that questioned God and God's goodness. He sought imaginary good beyond what God offered. He planted doubt about God's Word in Eve's mind, questioned God's love, denied God's honesty, and disputed God's goodness to His creation. He sowed discontent and ambition, tempting her with pleasure, possession, and

17

power (v. 6). Matthew Henry said, "Satan teaches man first to doubt and then to deny; he makes them skeptics first, and so by degrees making them atheists." Like the liberal theologian, Satan denied God's literal Word. He implied God was guilty of censorship by withholding knowledge that man and woman should possess. Like the cults, Eve added to God's Word, saying they couldn't *touch* the fruit. She then acted independently of God and did her own thing (Isaiah 53:6).

Eve lost the battle because she didn't believe God. Temptation was disguised, it was unexpected, and it came from a subordinate to mankind, who was to have dominion. Temptation took the form of an appeal to disobey God and to satisfy fleshly desires to gain knowledge God had prohibited. Evil existed, but God would have protected mankind from it had they obeyed. Eve gave some fruit to Adam and he also disobeyed God. Sin had compounded itself. Eve had been tricked by an angel of light (II Corinthians 11:3-4), but Adam sinned willfully (I Timothy 2:13-14). He loved the creature (his wife) more than his Creator. As head of his home, Adam not only failed to stop Eve from eating, but he joined her! The sinful nature and resulting death now would be passed on to all people (Romans 5:12; I Corinthians 15:22).

When Adam and Eve sinned, they lost innocence ("ignorance of evil"). Their "eyes were opened." In other words, man's conscience told him that he had done evil. He now saw things from a perverted position, from the viewpoint of a sinner. He learned about evil the hard way — and he wished he hadn't. His immediate reaction involved human effort to cover his sin. He sewed fig leaves together to cover his shame instead of confessing sin and seeking forgiveness. But fig leaves (like religion) merely hide sin. *God isn't into religion or fig leaves!* Jesus cursed the fig tree in Matthew just before He denounced the religious leaders of His day. He wants a *relationship* with His creatures. Now He will do something to insure that He has it!

GOD AND FIG FASHION

"And I will put enmity between you and the woman, and between your offspring and hers; he will crush your head, and you will strike his heel."

Genesis 3:15

SPORTSCASTER HARRY WISMER tried to cover up his mistake in a 1945 Army game. He told the radio audience: ". . . the ball is handed off to Glenn Davis. He's at the 30 . . . 20 . . . 10 . . . and Davis laterals to Doc Blanchard who goes in for a touchdown! . . . What a sportsman Davis is, tossing a lateral so his teammate could score!" In fact, Blanchard had the ball the whole time!

Our first parents covered up their sin with fig leaves instead of rushing to their Heavenly Father for forgiveness. But God, clothed in human form to communicate with His loved ones, sought out His created ones. The Lord may have been meeting regularly with them, but Adam and Eve became fearful, evasive, deceitful, cowardly, and biased against God after they sinned against Him. A. guilty conscience led them to run from God. Thankfully, a loving God sought out sinful mankind. Scripture clearly teaches that no one seeks Him first (Romans 3:11; John 15:16)!

Though he was created to be the leader, Adam became a follower. He blamed Eve and she blamed the serpent. Sin had divided the human family. Satan, a liar and a murderer from the beginning (John 8:44), enticed mankind to follow him.

A holy, just, and righteous God judged sin immediately. He cursed the slithering serpent to crawl on its belly. He judged Adam and Eve with death (spiritual separation immediately and physical death eventually). Adam would find work to be difficult, as weeds began to multiply exponentially. Too much leisure in his sinful state would spell trouble. Sorrow and frustration became part of his existence on the earth. Eve would have pain in childbirth. Con-

19

trary to most animal births, human childbirth is extremely painful and requires much assistance as a result of the curse. She would desire to overrule her husband. Adam would return to the dust from which he was created (not to the animal kingdom, for he hadn't evolved from an animal!). Both were now "like God" in that they knew good from evil. Yet, they became unable to do good or to resist evil. They became "slaves to sin" (Romans 7:14-25) and everyone to be born would inherit their same evil nature. Satan's lie that man could sin and get away with it was forever exposed.

The creation came under the curse of sin (Romans 8:20-22). Animals became carnivorous and the law of the jungle turned the ground red with blood. Satan became the "god of this age" (II Corinthians 4:4). The great conflict on earth between good and evil had begun.

God provided a covering for Adam and Eve's shame. He killed an animal and gave them animal skins to wear. When He banned them from Eden, they left behind the bloody sacrifice slain by God to cover them. An angel and a flaming sword guarded the tree of life (2:9).

Could man ever return to fellowship with God? God made a promise to provide one way only. He said the "seed of the woman" (not the man) would one day crush the head of the serpent (Satan). In the process, the heel of the woman's seed would be bruised. What could this mean? Today we have seen the conflict between Jesus (the offspring of the woman) and lost mankind (the offspring of the serpent). There is still no peace between God and those who refuse to believe and trust Him. Yet, God declared from the foundation of the world that Jesus would die for our sins and crush the serpent's head (Revelation 13:8). The animal skins symbolized the covering of His righteousness over our sin. The animal's blood symbolized His blood shed for all mankind. Only by the death and resurrection of the Son of God may we return to paradise! What a plan! What a promise!

MURDER ONE

Now Cain said to his brother Abel, "Let's go out to the field." And while they were in the field, Cain attacked his brother Abel and killed him.

Genesis 4:8

FORMER FOOTBALL GREAT O. J. Simpson was acquitted in the killing of two people in the early 1990s. Baltimore Ravens linebacker Ray Lewis was found not guilty of murder in a knife killing in the late 1990s. Evidence pointed to wealthy NBA player Jayson Williams in a February 14, 2002, shotgun murder, though the case was settled out of court.

Sometimes murders escape the judgment of human courts. But regardless of the prosecution of famous murders in history, Cain was apprehended and convicted by God Himself when he killed his brother Abel. Let's examine the circumstances.

Time had passed since the first parents were driven from Eden. Mankind had multiplied. Sons were born to Adam and Eve. Eve knew God's promise to send a Savior (3:15), and she probably believed she had produced him when Cain was born (4:1). Later, she gave birth to Abel. Abel kept sheep and Cain tilled the ground. (It's clear that early man was not a primitive caveman nor a prowler in the forest!)

The brothers brought offerings to the Lord. But Cain's heart wasn't right with God. He gave an offering out of religious formality. Abel brought his best to God. He loved God. Jesus said he was a prophet and set the date of his life near the beginning of the world (Luke 11:50-51). Abel may have warned Cain about his bad attitude toward God.

There must have been instruction that sinful man could approach God by faith with regular blood sacrifices. Abel did so (Hebrews 11:4). Cain lacked faith and one day he brought the fruit of his own efforts. He was not accepted by God. Cain's jealous anger turned into the premeditated murder of Abel, the first martyr (I John 3:12). When sought out and confronted by God, he was evasive and defiant. He claimed innocence and ignorance. But the God Who knows everything could not be deceived.

Cain belonged to Satan (I John 3:12). He worshipped in his own way and not God's prescribed way (Jude 11). His offering denied he was a sinner and separated from God. He offered his own works. Cain's judgment was to wander as a fugitive in the desert. He was sorry for the consequences of his sin, but not for the sin itself. Cain fled, married a close relative (this wasn't forbidden nor was it genetically risky at that time since there were no mutant genes) and fathered an ungodly line of offspring. Their guilt was eased by their pursuits in the world of travel, music, culture, and industry. Mankind began urban life without God. Lamech was the first polygamist. He was also a murderer and he boasted of it. Evil was advancing on earth. The world system was established to function without God, and it progressed.

In contrast, Seth fathered a Godly line of offspring which would lead to the Messiah promised in Genesis 3:15. The two lines of mankind would have conflict throughout history. Seth's line called on the Lord for forgiveness. The line of Cain continually rebelled. There was no human government to restrain anyone. Apart from God's intervention, peace on earth became an impossible dream.

A Line of Death

Altogether, Adam lived 930 years, and then he died.

Genesis 5:5

WE LIVE IN A WORLD of lawlessness, lust, and greed. Even such occasions as the 1993 threepeat by the Chicago Bulls resulted in two deaths, dozens of injuries, and hundreds of arrests in the "victory celebration" that followed. Magic Johnson lived in sexual sin and contracted AIDS, joining thousands of others who degrade their bodies sexually and with drugs. Mike Tyson, who enjoyed money and fame, sexually abused a beauty contestant and went to prison. The immorality of athletes and fans pollutes the sports pages every day.

Our world is in a mess because mankind is dead in sin! The written Word of God is consistent with His spoken promise to Adam and Eve. God promised they would die the very day they disobeyed Him! Spiritually, death (separation from God) came immediately. Physically, Adam lived 930 more years. The experience of death is common to all. Only Enoch, a preacher who was "translated" to heaven without dying (Hebrews 11:5), and Elijah (II Kings 2) are known exceptions. Death is a reality for all of us. Our hope is in being "born again" spiritually before we die (John 3:7) and therefore being resurrected by God after we die!

Chapter 5 records Adam's line of descendants. Evidently, Adam or a friend kept a written account of people. Possibly, Moses used this record as he wrote Genesis under the inspiration of the Holy Spirit. Children were born in the likeness of their father — sinners by nature and in practice (v. 3). No evolution (theistic or atheistic) occurred, for people reproduce people and animals reproduce animals. Details of creation, man's fall, God's promise, and man's dispersion could easily have been passed verbally from Adam to Lamech to Shem, to Jacob (four men)!

People lived to great ages before the flood. Possibly, a canopy of water vapor filtered out harmful ultraviolet rays, and increased barometric pressure and oxygen in the atmosphere made conditions ideal for long life and greater body size. Methuselah lived the longest (969 years). His name means "when he dies it shall be sent," and he pictures the great patience of God as man's lifestyle degenerated before the flood.

God used the term "man" to refer to male and female of humankind (vv. 1-2). From Genesis 5, we know the years from Adam to Noah ("rest") numbered 1,056 years. If there are no gaps in the Genesis 11 record, it was 891 more years until Abraham was born and from then until Jacob's birth was 160 years (21:5, 25:26). Jacob lived 147 years (47:28), during which he fathered Joseph (who died at 110), so he must have been born in 1915 B.C. (50:26). From the time Jacob entered Egypt until the Exodus (approximately 1445 B.C.) was 430 years (Exodus 12:40-41). The Bible gives the historical record that the earth and man are a little over 6,000 years old. Man's erroneous dating methods which say creation was millions of years ago do not stand up against God's Word.

Death came to all men because of Adam's sin. But reconciliation of man to God is by faith and ultimately guarantees victory over death (I Corinthians 15:22)! The Lord Jesus Christ created us and died to redeem us from the awful line of sin and death. We praise and thank Him for breaking that curse!

THE FLOOD

The Lord saw how great man's wickedness on the earth had become, and that every inclination of the thoughts of his heart was only evil all the time. The Lord was grieved that he had made man on the earth, and his heart was filled with pain. So the Lord said, "I will wipe mankind, whom I have created, from the face of the earth — men and animals, and creatures that move along the ground, and birds of the air — for I am grieved that I have made them." But Noah found favor in the eyes of the Lord.

Genesis 6:5-8

THE YEAR 1997 brought much bad weather early in the baseball season, including a June 21 deluge that swamped the field at County Stadium in Milwaukee. Brewers manager Phil Garner commented, "We've had a snowout, a rainout, and a coldout. And now we have a floodout. What I want to know is, When do the locusts come?"

A catastrophe stalked the earth. The mother of all rainouts was approaching. Possibly demon-possessed descendants of Seth had married ungodly daughters descended from Cain, and their descendants moved further from God (Genesis 6:1-2). Possibly, polygamy became rampant. God's Spirit drew men and women toward Himself, but they weren't responding. He had promised that the seed of the woman would produce a Redeemer to crush Satan, but if no one remained who sought God, the promise would be in jeopardy. So God served notice of a change in His way of dealing with mankind. He would limit man's opportunity to 120 years before bringing disaster upon earth. The warning was given.

The human race was totally depraved and the effects of sin multiplied exponentially. The long lifespans resulted in a massive increase in earth's population, even though the earth was only about 1,600 years old at the time. Those who rejected and rebelled against God dominated the world. Some were physically imposing and became renowned for their evil deeds. Some scholars believe marauding bands of violent men murdered and pillaged at will. Society degenerated rapidly as mankind turned far from God. Anarchy and terrorism must have prevailed. Henry Morris says the sin-disease progressed so far that "only a global bath of water from the windows of heaven could purge and cleanse the fevered earth."

A man named Noah ("this one will comfort") walked with God in righteousness. Noah was an extremely intelligent man and he found grace (favor) with God because of his faith in God and His Word. The first use of "grace" in Scripture concerns Noah. It was a wonderful revelation of the nature of God! But Noah was in the vast minority. God gave Noah the technical instruction for the construction of a huge, wooden ship. It contained 1.4 million cubic feet on three levels and equaled the length of 522 railroad box cars. It was the early 1900s before another boat this big was built! By faith, Noah obeyed God and built the ark on dry land at a time when it had never rained (Hebrews 11:7). Noah worked for 120 years on the Ark. Enoch preached during that time until God took him to heaven (Hebrews 11:5). This should have been a warning of God's intervention in human affairs. Methuselah ("when he dies it shall come") was another warning to lost mankind. But man wouldn't listen. Noah was probably considered a fool, a laughing stock. People lived long lives and death was far from their minds. Satan ruled over a lost world and he was turning it into what has been called a "province of hell."

After 20 years of labor on the ark, Shem was born to Noah and his wife. What an encouragement! God would sustain him and keep His creation alive. Later, two more sons were born. There was hope in the promises of God!

Jesus verified the historicity of the great flood of Noah's day and encouraged us to study it because conditions on earth would be similar just prior to His return (Matthew 24:37-39). We ignore these conditions at our peril. God is merciful, but His tolerance of sin in His world has a limit.

GOD'S PATIENCE IS EXHAUSTED

. . . All the springs of the great deep burst forth, and the floodgates of the heavens were opened. And rain fell on the earth forty days and forty nights.

Genesis 7:12

PATIENCE WITH DEVELOPING players is a virtue. They must be given time to improve. A wise coach is patient, especially with young players. Nevertheless, there comes a time when every player must produce to stay on the field!

God shows much patience to mankind, but His patience with our sin has a limit. His patience was finally exhausted in Noah's day. After over 100 years of preaching and building, Noah entered the ark at God's direction! God caused the first mass animal migration in history. Two of every kind (with some extras for sacrifice and rapid multiplication) entered the ark. It must have taken a week to load, but God waited before shutting and sealing the door. His gentle striving with man at that time was over. Only Noah and his family were saved — safe in the ark. It would be over a year before they would again set foot on dry land!

The flood was sudden, devastating and worldwide. (If it was only local, the ark was unnecessary.) The "spring of the great deep burst forth." Evidently, great seismic shifts of earth's plates, underwater volcanic eruptions spewing out hot mantle, subterranean geysers, and/or great uplift of the sea floor caused spillage of sea water over the land. Some believe God tilted earth on its axis at that time. The floodgates of the heavens were opened and the canopy of water descended. A catastrophe resulted. Every land creature, including man, perished. Entire forests were wiped away in enormous mudslides. Currents laid down layer upon layer of sediment as they rapidly swept back and forth on the earth. Water covered the highest mountains

27

by at least 20 feet (v. 20). On every continent, the large numbers of fossil, coal, and oil deposits remind us of God's terrible judgment on sin. He wiped man and animals from the face of the earth. They speak a silent warning today!

The enormity of the flood has been overlooked or forgotten by many people. But its lesson is clear: This is God's world to preserve or destroy. He will not tolerate sin indefinitely. He is a holy God and man cannot get away with sin against Him. But He also provides a way of escape. As God invited Noah into the ark to be saved, He invites people today to come to the cross of Jesus Christ. There is one door to salvation, and Jesus is that door. But you must enter now, before it's too late!

THE WATER RECEDES

But God remembered Noah and all the wild animals and the livestock that were with him in the ark, and he sent a wind over the earth, and the waters receded.

Genesis 8:1

NOAH HAD PLENTY OF TIME to spend with his family on the ark! For 150 days, no land was visible. The ark struck ground on the mountains of Ararat (in modern Turkey). Before the flood, there was evidently one land mass (Genesis 1:9). Psalm 104:7-9 describes what happened after the flood: "But at your rebuke the waters fled, at the sound of your thunder they took to flight; they flowed over the mountains, they went down into the valleys, to the place you assigned for them. You set a boundary they cannot cross; never again will they cover the earth." Evidently, continental drift and plate techtonics continued rapidly and massive runoff carved great valleys like the Grand Canyon in the sediments laid down by the flood. The great weight of the water pressed vegetation into coal and organic material into oil. Some trees became petrified before they could decay. Fossils were formed with simple marine invertebrates generally in bottom layers and land vertebrates in top layers.

The changed atmosphere during the flood altered climate and weather conditions, causing polar ice caps and a later Ice Age. In Siberia, hundreds of thousands of woolly mammoths drowned in mudslides, which then froze. Huge ice sheets in northern latitudes covered one-third of earth's surface for probably 700 years! Job may have written about such changed conditions in Job 38:29-30. "From whose womb comes the ice? Who gives birth to the frost from the heavens when the waters become hard as stone, when the surface of the deep is frozen?"

The earth had been drastically changed (II Peter 3:6-7). Much of earth became a desolate wilderness, some-

29

times very windy and chilly. Dark clouds occasionally threatened more rain! The oceans were larger, more land was uninhabitable due to uplifted mountain ranges, and volcanoes and earthquakes reflected the instability of the planet. The land animals multiplied and spread out rapidly via land bridges until each kind found environments suitable to them. Inbreeding allowed for variations within kinds (not evolution into new kinds). Some kinds were eventually unable to endure the changing conditions on earth and became extinct, especially during the Ice Age.

God remembered Noah and his family in the ark. He began again to act on their behalf. Noah sent out a raven, (which could live on almost anything) and it flew back and forth over the water. Then he sent a dove, which wouldn't land on a dead animal body and was very selective in food choices. After three tours, the dove didn't return and Noah knew the water had receded. After 371 days, it was time to disembark!

Grateful for God's preservation, Noah offered one-seventh of all clean animals as a sacrifice on an "altar" he built. God was pleased with Noah. He promised to never again curse the ground nor to destroy every living thing. He promised predictable seasons. All mankind still acted as depraved sinners from birth. The flood did not improve man! But the God of all grace still saves all who acknowledge their sin and trust Him!

STARTING OVER

"I established my covenant with you: Never again will all life be cut off by the waters of a flood; never again will there be a flood to destroy the earth."

Genesis 9:11

THE RED SOX' Lefty O'Doul had to start over. He gave up a record 13 runs in one inning on July 7, 1923. The Red Sox removed him from the mound and changed his position. He developed into a hard-hitting outfielder who enjoyed a notable career!

God "started over" with eight people after the flood. But world conditions became vastly different from conditions before the flood! All geological age indications were obliterated by the tremendous currents that laid down layers of sediment. The earth's surface was torn by deep canyons and huge mountains were uplifted. Severe weather became common, at times threatening other floods. Strong winds, extremes in cold and heat, and natural disasters raked the earth. Animals now feared man (v. 2), a fact which has saved some kinds from extinction! Refuges are needed today to save other kinds from our wanton killing!

God approved eating the meat of some animals (v. 3), but not the blood. He also instituted human government, with the power of capital punishment to protect mankind. Life is sacred and man isn't to murder. If one murders, the *government* (not an individual) has the right to take the life of the murderer.

The sign of God's covenant with Noah is the rainbow ("battle bow"). God will never totally flood earth again, though local floods have killed thousands. The next time earth is judged, it will be by fire (Matthew 24:37-39; II Peter 3:10-11). Though earth's conditions have changed, one thing remains the same: The nature of man is unchanged. Noah is about to illustrate.

NOAH FUMBLES THE BALL

When Noah awoke from his wine and found out what his youngest son had done to him, he said, "Cursed be Canaan! The lowest of slaves will he be to his brothers."

Genesis 9:24-25

OLE MISS COACH FRANK MASON lost respect because of his tactic in a 1907 game. On a bitterly cold day, Mason let his team drink gallons of whisky-laced coffee to keep warm on the sidelines. By the second half, the Rebels were fumbling the football, missing tackles, and muffing punts. They "staggered" to a 15-0 loss.

Alcohol caused righteous Noah to lose respect after the flood. He planted a vineyard and one day he drank too much wine. Stumbling into his tent in the warm climate, Noah carelessly discarded his clothes. His son Ham "intently gazed upon" the scene, went outside, and "told with delight" Noah's moral lapse to his brothers. This lack of respect for the authority of his father was revealed when Ham made light of him. He passed the root sin of lust and rebellion on to his descendants. Though it's not stated, it's possible that Canaan, Ham's son, first saw Noah and told his father.

Both Shem and Japheth respected and honored their father, even in his drunken condition. They kept their eyes from his nakedness and covered him with a blanket. When Noah awoke and was told what happened, he pronounced prophetic blessings on Shem (ancestor of Israel) and Japheth (ancestor of Greek and Roman civilizations). But he pronounced a prophetic curse upon the Canaanites. Moses recorded this prophecy as Israel was about to enter the land of Canaan. The Canaanites lived very degraded lives, noted for immorality, sex-centered religions, and human sacrifices. Noah had foreseen this behavior in his day. The curse he pronounced applied to those listed in Genesis 10:15-19, and included the Sodomites,

33

Gomorrahans, "cities of the plain" (destroyed in Genesis 19), Amorites, Phoenicians, and Carthaginians — all descendants of Canaan. It ended with the Roman destruction of Carthage in 146 b.c., 2,000 years after Noah prophesied!

After living for 950 years, Noah died. Matthew Henry writes, "Noah lived to see two worlds, but, being an heir of righteousness, which is by faith, when he died he went to see a world better than either." He wasn't perfect, but he was saved by the grace of God!

THE NATIONS

This is the account of Shem, Ham, and Japheth, Noah's sons, who themselves had sons after the flood.

Genesis 10:1

THE NATIONS OF THE WORLD assemble every four years for the Olympic Games. From every corner of the earth, the best competitors strive for a gold medal in various sports. The opening parade is a magnificent display of some 10,000 athletes and the diversity of their countries.

Where did these nations originate? All came from the three sons of Noah! All are members of one race — the human race! Genesis 10 stands alone in the historical records as an overview of Noah's descendants after the "Great Flood." There is no document of ancient history that is even close to its authority and detail. Archaeological discoveries of the last 150 years have confirmed its accuracy.

The time span of the nations in Genesis 10 extends beyond the events of chapter 11, for chapter 10 speaks of many clans and languages (v. 5, 20, 31) and chapter 11 traces the line of Shem to Abraham. Because of intermarriage, some groups can even trace their ancestry to more than one of Noah's sons! One of Shem's descendants, Pelag, was born just after the division of the people at Babel (v. 25). His name means "division."

Noah's youngest son, Shem, fathered the nation of Israel and some of the Arabian peoples. It was through Shem that Abraham and, ultimately, Jesus Christ would come. Eber is the origin of the name "Hebrew."

Noah's oldest son, Japheth, fathered the nations of Europe and Asia. They became known as "Gentiles" in the New Testament.

Noah's middle son, Ham, fathered nations of Africa and part of Arabia. Descendants of Ham founded the first three great civilizations upon the earth: Babylonian, Assyrian,

35

and Egyptian. Thirty of the 70 nations mentioned in Genesis 10 come from Ham ("black"). The black man was prominent early in history. One noteworthy descendent of Ham was Nimrod, son of Cush (Ham's eldest son). Nimrod's name means "let us rebel." Henry Morris theorizes that Cush resented Noah's curse upon Canaan more and more as time passed and raised Nimrod to lead a planned, organized rebellion against God's purpose for mankind. Nimrod was a "mighty hunter" of animals and/or of people. He organized a central world system in defiance of God. Nimrod became a monarch "against" the Lord. Satan himself was behind this effort to govern the world independently of God. The conflict of the ages was heating up!

Man Vs. God — Again

*So the Lord scattered them from there over all the earth,
and they stopped building the city.*

Genesis 11:8

SOMETIMES MANKIND REPEATS his errors and things
appear to go from bad to worse. In 1932, a ball skipped
through the legs of White Sox outfielder Smead Jolly and
he was charged with an error. The ball hit the wall and
caromed back through his legs for lapse #2! Finally, Smead
picked up the ball and threw it over the third baseman's
head for error #3 as the runner circled the bases. Fortu-
nately, he was only charged with two official errors!

Man repeated his errors against God in Genesis 11,
another pivot point in history. Human beings continued
their rebellion against a holy God, even though it was possibly only 100 years since the flood. Man's rebellious behavior caused the Lord to intervene again in the affairs of
earth.

God planned that people scatter, give Him glory, and
worship Him under a theocracy. But humans wanted to
stay together in deliberate opposition to God and to make
a name for themselves. Wicked men devised a self-suffi-
cient society independent of God, evidently under the dic-
tatorship of Nimrod. Such plans constituted self-worship
and led to actual Satan-worship, for Satan was the deceiver behind it all!

Nimrod built Babylon and apparently the Tower of
Babel as a rallying point for man's pride and unity. Babel
means "gate of God" and the Tower was a skyscraper. It
was also a worship center, a "ziggurat." Ziggurats had
circular stairs around them and people worshipped the
sun, moon, and stars from the top. This worship was for-
malized, with the signs of the zodiac engraved throughout. Sometimes, human sacrifices were offered upon zig-

gurats. The Tower of Babel became a center of paganism as man worshipped the creation instead of the Creator (Romans 1:25). Possibly, Nimrod deified himself as the god "Marduk," for Babylonian accounts say every brick had that name inscribed.

Mankind is very creative, competent, and powerful. We can fly to the moon or descend deep into the ocean! But the evil that man can do, unified under Satan, is almost unimaginable. Apart from God, man's unity is terribly destructive.

God erected an insurmountable barrier to our unity. All people spoke one language, though no one knows which one. Speaking within the Trinity, God said, "Let us go down and confuse their language so they will not understand each other." Suddenly, the bricklayers couldn't understand their foremen, who couldn't understand the architects! The unity that prideful man considered his greatest strength was destroyed by God in a moment! Supernaturally, God implanted various languages in different people!

Language remains the greatest barrier between humans today. Each family group became a tribe and scattered by language to various parts of the world. Some creative groups (Chinese, Babylonians, Greeks) worked out new alphabets to fit their languages, while others never learned to write their new language. The former groups made great strides in science, math, and culture, while the latter never progressed. As Dr. H. C. Leupold says, "The 3,000-5,000 plus languages on earth are a monument not to human ingenuity, but to human sin."

Inbreeding populations led to loss of genetic information and variation between the tribes. The "nations" were begun. Future wars were inevitable, but worldwide apostasy under Satan was stopped. Out of the scattered nations, God would soon select one nation (Israel) through which He would bless the world. His plan will be accomplished!

THE MESSIANIC LINE

Terah lived 205 years, and he died in Haran.
Genesis 11:32

SONS INHERIT BOTH PHYSICAL CHARACTERISTICS and skills from their fathers. They also inherit baseball aptitude, though the environment plays a significant role. Many sons of Major League players have reached the professional level and four men have even managed their own sons in the majors. Connie Mack, Yogi Berra, Cal Ripken, Sr., and Hal McRae have been blessed with this privilege. McRae told *Sports Illustrated* that he probably had seen his son Brian play more games since becoming manager than he saw in the rest of his son's life!

The human bloodlines of Jesus our Messiah, who was totally man and totally God, are carefully recorded in God's Word. The first 11 chapters of Genesis cover over 2,000 years of history, while chapters 12 to 50 cover only 350 years. In chapter 11, God reveals Christ's ancestors from Shem to Abraham. Both are in the bloodline of Mary, mother of Jesus. Apparently Shem kept the genealogical records of 10:1-11:9, Terah added 11:10-27a, and Isaac picked up the records from 11:27b onward. Morris says there is no indication that the writer meant to convey any existing gaps in the record. There is no indisputable evidence in historical records of Egypt, Samaria, or any ancient nations to force the insertion of gaps in these genealogies.

It's noteworthy that man's lifespan decreased after the flood. The longest-living person born after the flood was Eber, after whom the Hebrews were named. Whatever the reason (increased radiation reaching earth, accelerated aging, inadequate nourishment, inbreeding or increased stress), God cut man's time on earth. Every person must decide to follow God or to abandon God, and we live with the consequences of our choice for eternity. We must choose to follow God within our limited life span. It's so brief that James 4:14 calls it a "mist."

Ur became a wicked, prosperous city near the Persian Gulf. The name Ur means "the moon goddess," and the culture was very idolatrous, especially worshipping the moon. Terah, once a God-fearing man, worshipped idols in Ur in his later years (Joshua 24:2). He traveled 600 miles to Haran ("delay"), a northwest trading crossroads in Syria. There he died. Abram ("exalted father") or Abraham ("father of a multitude") was born in 2165 bc. When he was 75, he left Haran (Genesis 12:4). It may have been 367 years since the flood and 267 years since Babel. God's plan was in motion and His promises were going to be fulfilled.

GOD CALLS A MAN

The LORD had said to Abram, "Leave your country, your people and your father's household and go to the land I will show you.

"I will make you into a great nation and I will bless you; I will make your name great, and you will be a blessing.

I will bless those who bless you and whoever curses you I will curse;

And all peoples on earth will be blessed through you."

Genesis 12:1-3

WHAT A THRILL to be called to the big leagues! Ryan Glynn got the call at noon on May 16, 1999, when the Texas Rangers summoned him from Oklahoma City. He had just completed a workout on an off day and was planning to work the radar gun during his team's Triple A game. When the call came, he raced home for some clothes, hurried to the airport, flew to Arlington, Texas, where the clubhouse attendants had already sewn his name on the back of his uniform, and went to the bullpen. Ten minutes later, he was headed to the mound for his first Major League appearance! Just 4[1,2] hours after being called, he struck out the legendary Cal Ripken, Jr.!

The judgment of Babel did not cause men to return to God. The resulting nations continued to avoid Him, sinking lower and lower into moral rebellion. Therefore, God tried a new approach. He began to work through a man and a nation and He issued a call to a man named Abram.

God first called Abram from Ur (Acts 7:2-4), where he was living in a pagan household. Abram traveled 600 miles to Haran with his father Terah, who was an idol-worshiper like most other people on earth (Joshua 24:2). Though he couldn't have known it at the time, leaving Ur probably saved his life, for the city was destroyed in 2004 bc! Abram stopped in Haran (in a state of incomplete obedience) un-

41

til Terah died. Both Haran and Ur were centers of worship of the moon god, Sin (Sumerian "Nanna"). Abram's delay delayed God's blessing.

In Genesis 12, God repeated His call to Abram to go to the Promised Land. This time, 75 year-old Abram obeyed more fully (12:4), traveling 400 additional miles to Canaan. But his obedience was still partial, as he took his nephew Lot along! Much grief results from his incomplete obedience.

God unconditionally promised Abram blessing, influence, fame, protection, and a homeland for his posterity. Anyone who blessed Abram would be blessed. Anyone who mistreated Abram would be aligning himself against Abram's God and would be cursed. Abram was already wealthy. Though he knew generally where he was to go, he wasn't told a specific site in Canaan (Hebrews 11:8). When he arrived at Shechem, near the center of Canaan, the Lord Jesus Christ appeared to Abram. There, Abram built an altar near a well-known landmark (a huge tree). This was the first place of true worship in Canaan. Nomadic Abram built another altar 35 miles south at Bethel, where he called on God for guidance and help. God answered, providing daily food, guidance and protection as Abram learned to walk by faith. God even announced the gospel in advance to Abram (Galatians 3:6-9)!

Abram is probably the world's most famous man. This man is our spiritual father through Isaac, the son of the promise God made to him. At first, Abram was weak in faith. He had to learn to rely on God, just as we must learn to live by faith! Over the years, he learned valuable lessons. He remains an example for God's children today!

INFLUENCE THROWN AWAY

So Pharaoh summoned Abram. "What have you done to me?" he said. "Why didn't you tell me she was your wife? Why did you say, 'She is my sister,' so that I took her to be my wife? Now then, here is your wife. Take her and go! "

Genesis 12:19

A FEW YEARS AGO, two Florida teenagers broke into a baseball card store and stole $45,000 worth of sports collectibles. In sorting through the loot, they evidently overlooked a signature on an old baseball and threw it into a dumpster. After being arrested, the teens told their story. Authorities rushed to the dumpster, but it was too late. The ball, autographed by Babe Ruth, had been thrown into the incinerator!

Abram threw away something far more valuable than a Babe Ruth baseball. He lost his influence on the Egyptian world because he lied about Sarai, his wife. Here's how it happened:

There was a food shortage in Canaan and Abram panicked. He took matters into his own hands, left the land of promise, and went to Egypt (a symbol of the world). He should have trusted God by faith and stayed where God assigned him. His compromise brought great trouble with it. Out of his element as a nomadic shepherd, he re-entered the world's high civilization.

At first, the prosperity of Egypt made Abram's decision seem right. But he hadn't foreseen that the polytheistic, cruel, and immoral Egyptians would lust after Sarai, his beautiful wife (who was also his half-sister). Much earlier, they had agreed to tell a half- truth about her identity in such a situation (Genesis 20:12-13). But a half-truth is a total lie! The deception got Sarai into the Pharaoh's harem and brought Abram much wealth as payment. Though Pharaoh hadn't yet had time to sleep with Sarai, both she

43

and Abram must have spent many sleepless nights wishing they had trusted God in Canaan — famine or no famine!

God's people were stuck — but God was not. He sent a great plague upon the house of Pharaoh, who realized that Abram and Sarai's God was protecting them. All Pharaoh could do to save himself was to get rid of them, though he had lost all respect for both and probably would have killed them if he didn't fear their God!

It was a long journey home. Abram and Sarai had thrown away their influence for good in the Egyptian world. They had also likely lost the respect of their own servants and Abram's nephew, Lot.

Distrust of God and deceitfulness causes us to lose respect. The end never justifies the means! We never get away with sin without paying the consequences. The very ones Abram should have influenced for God now rebuked and despised him.

Read Genesis 13:1-13

Lot's Sad Choice

Abram lived in the land of Canaan, while Lot lived among the cities of the plain and pitched his tents near Sodom. Now the men of Sodom were wicked and were sinning greatly against the Lord.

Genesis 13:12-13

FORMER MAJOR LEAGUER Tom Herr made a good choice when he denied his desire to manage a pro team so he could stay involved with his son in high school baseball. "I think I'm making the right decision for my son. I'm not sure it's the right decision for me," he said. Herr's self-sacrifice is rare in the "me-first" culture of America!

Life would have been better for Lot had he used the wisdom and unselfish logic of Tom Herr. Lot had followed Abram back to Bethel — the last place Abram had built an altar and enjoyed sweet fellowship with the Lord. Once he was back in the will of God, the Lord reappeared to him. Once again in the land of promise, Abram prayed and evidently rediscovered the joy of his salvation (I John 1:9). But circumstances had changed. Abram and Lot were now very rich. In fact, Abram was the Bill Gates of his day! Lot, who should have been left in Haran years ago (Genesis 12:1), evidently lost respect for Abram and conflict resulted. The friction between these two believers would cause the Canaanites to lose respect for both of them! Separation was inevitable.

Abram graciously let Lot choose where he wanted to live. Looking east, Lot chose the Jordanian plain, where there were five prosperous cities. At that time, this plain was well watered and fertile. Though Lot probably knew of the wickedness of the people there, he chose the "creature comforts" they offered. He was still under the influence of the trip to Egypt (v. 10). The wealth of this world was dividing Abram and Lot.

45

At first, Lot lived near Sodom. He wanted the spiritual blessings of God and the carnal advantages of fellowship with the world. But neither God nor the world will let that happen! We eventually must choose between them. Soon, Lot moved into Sodom (Genesis 14:12). Then, he became a local leader in Sodom (Genesis 19:1). Tragedy was soon to follow for his entire family.

ABRAM REASSURED

All the land that you see I will give to you and your off-spring forever.

Genesis 13:15

WE OFTEN NEED the encouragement of others. Ex-Cubs manager Don Baylor was no exception. In April 2002, Baylor arrived at Wrigley Field to hear of Sammy Sosa's renewed feud with the Giants' Barry Bonds. One hour before game time, several players aired grievances. Then, the Cubs went out on a 40-degree night and fell behind by 12 runs before losing 12-4 to the Giants. Chicago General Manager Andy McPhail moved quickly to quiet talk of Baylor's firing, calling such talk "not worth the ink that's needed to print this sentence." It's nice to have the reassurance of the boss when times are tough! Unfortunately, it must have been only talk, for Baylor was fired in July of the same year!

After Lot departed from him, Abram was reassured by God himself! God's reassurance is more than mere words! Abram had learned a hard lesson, but he was back in God's will. He was dwelling in the Promised Land and Lot had separated from him. The Lord spoke, confirming that the land was his and he would have great numbers of descendants.

For most of human history, Abram's descendants through Isaac haven't owned the Promised Land. One day, they'll possess it all! God has given it to the Hebrews! It was a beautiful land and one of the Dead Sea Scrolls describes this section of Genesis in Abram's first-person account. He built another altar in Mamre ("richness"), near the future city of Hebron ("communion"). Abram lived there for some time. He grew stronger in faith and God planned to bless him abundantly.

THE VICTOR AND THE SPOILS

When Abram heard that his relative had been taken captive, he called out the 318 trained men born in his household and went in pursuit as far as Dan. During the night Abram divided his men to attack them and he routed them, pursuing them as far as Hobah, north of Damascus.

Genesis 14:14-15

IT WASN'T THE FIRST BASEBALL WAR, but when Roger Clemens threw a bat at Mike Piazza in 2001, it set off quite a fervor in New York. The tension continued into 2002 when Clemens came to bat against the Mets' Shawn Estes in an interleague game. Estes threw a pitch behind Clemens, sending him a message without hitting him. Then Shawn hit a home run to help win the game!

After Abram had lived peacefully in Mamre for many years, a regional war took place between the pagan nations of the Middle East. Four northeastern nations from ancient Persia (Iran) and Babylon (Iraq) attacked five nations near the Dead Sea, probably because of the rich mineral deposits and fertile land in the area. The campaign was overwhelming and brutal. Lot was among those captured by the invaders. It was the first recorded war in history.

Abram had to make a decision. Should he stay neutral or should he rescue his nephew? He took 318 warriors and, though heavily outnumbered, pursued the enemy for over 150 miles. Attacking at night, he surprised Lot's captors and recovered many captives and their possessions. Though he was only trying to rescue his nephew, Abram became a military hero!

Two men now enter the stage of history. They come at different times and they have different agendas. The first man, the King of Sodom, approached Abram immediately after his great victory. He offered to give him all the mate-

49

rial goods recovered by Abram in the raid. But Abram knew that dealing with this wicked man could be dangerous. He wisely refused to receive anything from the sodomite king. This pagan king couldn't say he'd made Abram wealthy and steal the glory from the living God! Abram's allegiance was now totally to the Creator of heaven and earth. His failure in Egypt had changed his attitude about accepting riches from pagan idolaters! Abram passed this test of faith and it set the stage for God's greatest revelation!

The second man to meet Abram after his victory was Melchizedek, king and priest of ancient Jerusalem (Salem). This man blessed Abram, who respectfully gave him one-tenth of everything he possessed. Melchizedek is mentioned again in the Scriptures. He is mentioned 900 years later by David (Psalm 110:4) and 1,900 years later by the writer of Hebrews. Ancient Hebrew tradition says he was actually the patriarch Shem, who had migrated to Jerusalem under divine guidance carrying the genealogical records. This may or may not be true, but Melchizedek is a type of Jesus Christ. His name means "King of Righteousness" (Hebrews 7:2) and his title (King of Salem) means "King of Peace." Abram recognized him as his spiritual superior. Melchizedek knew the living God and he interceded (acting as a priest) for those who wanted to know God. He was not a pantheist addicted to nature worship or a polytheist like the Canaanites around him. His priesthood had no recorded beginning or ending. It resembled Christ's priesthood (Hebrews 7:17), which was superior to the future priesthood of Aaron.

Like the king of Sodom, Satan is always ready to steal glory from God after every victory. Abram wouldn't let him and neither should we. Like Melchizedek, Jesus is always ready to give us blessing, help, and strength when we're tempted. He is a great High Priest and he always intercedes to the Father on our behalf! We must trust Him in victory as well as in defeat!

A VISION AND A COVENANT

After this, the word of the LORD came to Abram in a vision: "Do not be afraid, Abram. I am your shield, your very great reward."

Genesis 15:1

WORDS CONVEY SPECIFIC MEANINGS. Old-time baseball writers often used colorful words to describe the game. Many of these words are no longer in use. Fans were once called "pluggers," a bad play was a "foozle," and a fly ball was a "skyscraper." The dugout was the "dog kennel" and a curve ball was a "mackerel." We've lost some of the game's color by the loss of such descriptive words.

God has given man the ability to understand words in order to communicate His will. Therefore, man can respond with obedience and praise. Genesis 15 is the story of God's plan communicated in a vision with one word. That word is "covenant." It means a "solemn binding agreement." Abram watched as the vision lasted all day and into the night. The vision traversed down through the centuries all the way to the Lord Jesus Christ, who called himself "I Am" (John 8:56-58)!

The Lord Jesus first called Himself "I Am" in Genesis 15. He is a "Shield, a very great Reward." Abram was living in a pagan land with enemies on every side. The kings he had just defeated could return at any time. But God (his "Shield") said, "Fear not" for the first time. He was Abram's reward for his faith. Abram had rejected the rewards offered by Sodom's king. God Himself was enough reward.

A deep concern weighed upon Abram. He didn't understand how his offspring could inherit anything because he was childless! According to the law at that time (Code of Hammurabi), his chief servant (Eliezer) would obtain his inheritance if he had no son. God promised Abram a

51

son and offspring as plentiful as the stars! Abram believed God! He "placed confidence in God," "relied upon God," and "was persuaded to trust God." It was more than intellectual assent. God counted (chashad = "imputed") Abram righteous on the basis of this belief! This is the great principle of salvation! Abram wasn't counted righteous because of anything he did. He simply believed God. Genesis 15:6 is quoted three times in the New Testament (Romans 4:3, Galatians 3:6, James 2:23). God's principle of saving lost men and women is found here. Abram's spiritual offspring (all who believe in the Lord Jesus Christ) are compared to the stars. His physical offspring (Israel) are numerous as dust particles (Genesis 13:16). What a promise!

Abram requested a sign from God. God marked out His covenant in the same way ancient agreements were sealed. Two parties agreeing together passed between halves of a slain animal (Jeremiah 34:18). They vowed to keep the covenant or be slain like the animal!

Abram killed three animals and two birds and cut them in halves. Nothing happened until nightfall. In the meantime, Abram drove off pesky vultures (symbolic of Satan, who always tries to disrupt God's plan). At dusk, God put Abram into a deep sleep (symbolic of Israel's 400 years of oppression in Egypt). The reason for the long delay was God's patience with the pagans (Amorites) who lived in the Promised Land (v 16). He doesn't want anyone to perish, but to repent (II Peter 3:9). His patience in delaying judgment is very great — but it's limited!

Finally, God Himself walked between the animal halves. His promise was unconditional. It was not a pact between two equals. A firepot (suffering of Jesus) and a torch (glory) pictured the sequence to come many years later.

God gave to Abram and his heirs (Israel) all land between the River of Egypt and the Euphrates. He needed no help from Abram to fulfill the promise. Unfortunately, Abram and Sarai were about to get in the way, causing themselves and the world much grief!

An Attempt to Manage God's Team

Now Sarai, Abram's wife, had borne him no children. But she had an Egyptian maidservant named Hagar, so she said to Abram, "The Lord has kept me from having children. Go, sleep with my maidservant; perhaps I can build a family through her."

Genesis 16:1-2

FEW PLAYERS SEE THE ENTIRE PICTURE of most games, but managers must consider every detail before making decisions. Conflict results when players make decisions that aren't theirs to make. Writer Dave Boswell reported that the Orioles' Reggie Jackson once stole second base against the wishes of manager Earl Weaver. Because he wasn't thinking like Weaver, a managerial genius, Weaver let him know it. The opponent intentionally walked powerful Lee May, and, because the next hitter struggled against the pitcher, Earl had to use a pinch hitter too early in the game. Weaver did not appreciate any player's attempts to manage his team!

Seventy-five-year-old Sarai's faith weakened and she sought to "manage God's team." Feeling the "shame" of childlessness, Sarai suggested 86 year-old Abram have sex with her servant Hagar so the resulting child could fulfill God's promise. Abram unwisely listened to his wife, just as Adam had done centuries earlier. Manipulation and man's worldly wisdom always bring trouble. Compromise complicates and brings grief!

Sarai did wrong to Hagar, the Egyptian servant girl who was probably acquired on their previous trip to Egypt. Hagar despised Sarai when she discovered she was pregnant. So, Sarai blamed Abram! Furthermore, she mistreated Hagar and Abram allowed it. He was failing to lead his own household and he was learning that polygamy causes problems!

53

Hagar fled back toward Egypt. But God loved Hagar and the angel of the LORD (Jesus Christ) met her, sent her back to Sarai, and promised her many descendants. She said, "You are the God who sees me (El Roi)." There was a reunion when Hagar shared her story of meeting God. Abram named the child Ishmael ("God hears") to signify that God had heard Hagar in her misery.

God predicted Ishmael's future. He would be wild, unruly, and warlike, living in conflict with everyone around him. The descendants of Ishmael (Arabs) have fulfilled this prophecy. Most of them hate Israel and would like to eliminate them from existence. Such was the consequence of trying to "manage God's team."

The next 13 years aren't recorded in Scripture. There is no recorded word from God. Abram prospered, there was peace in the land, and, evidently, Abram and Sarai gave up any thought of having their own child. God hadn't forgotten, however!

THE SIGN

You are to undergo circumcision, and it will be the sign of the covenant between me and you.

Genesis 17:11

A GAME IN 1981 SIGNIFIED THAT CAL RIPKEN, JR., could become an "iron man" of baseball endurance. As a minor league third baseman, Cal played every inning of the longest professional game in history. The Triple A game between his Rochester team and Pawtucket was suspended on April 19 after eight hours and seven minutes! It was completed in 18 minutes on June 23 when Pawtucket scored a run in the bottom of the 33rd inning for a 3-2 victory!

God appeared to Abram for the fifth time when the patriarch was 99 years old. He wanted to remind Abram to walk by faith and not by sight as he had often done. The LORD confirmed His covenant with a sign. That sign was circumcision — the cutting away of the loose skin at the end of the penis. Like baptism today (Colossians 2:11), circumcision was an outward sign of an inward reality. It symbolized putting away the impurity of natural man and dependence upon God for life. Abram's initial reaction was to laugh at the promise of a son through 90-year old Sarai. But immediately (Romans 4:18-22), his doubt turned to faith and he circumcised every male in the household! John McArthur writes, "The symbolism (of circumcision) had to do with the need to cut away sin and be cleansed. It was the male organ which most clearly demonstrated the depth of depravity because it carried the seed that produced depraved sinners. Thus, circumcision symbolized the need for a profoundly deep cleansing to reverse the effects of depravity."

God revealed Himself and what He wanted of Abram by degrees. He called Himself "El Shaddai" or "God Almighty," stressing His power. God changed Abram's name ("exalted father") to Abraham ("father of a multitude") before Isaac was born. God promised Abraham and his descendants the whole land of Canaan (v 8) and more (Genesis 15:18-21). If Israel would only trust God, she would easily conquer all land from the River of Egypt to the Euphrates!

God changed Sarai's ("contentious") name to Sarah ("princess"). Her womb was a tomb, but God brought life from death when she bore Isaac ("He laughs"), through whom all the promises are fulfilled. Isaac's name forever reminded Abraham of God's faithfulness. Ishmael was blessed and he fathered 12 tribal rulers (Genesis 25:12-18). But God's covenant was through Isaac and not Ishmael.

Spiritually speaking, all who believe in Jesus Christ are children of Abraham, for Abraham believed God and rejoiced in God's promise to send Jesus (John 8:56). Though the nation (Israel) fell away (became "apostate"), God remained faithful to His promise. There has always been a few (a "remnant") who remained faithful to Him.

Strengthened Faith

"Is anything too hard for the LORD? I will return to you at the appointed time next year and Sarah will have a son."
Genesis 18:14

IN 1956, NO ONE would have believed that 16-year-old Joe Torre would achieve Major League notoriety. He was fat and slow and seemed to have none of his brother Frank's talent. Joe was one year away from working as a page on Wall Street for $33 a week. But Frank got two tickets to game five of the World Series and gave them to his brother. Don Larson pitched a perfect game that day and Joe's vision was renewed.

The Bible is brutally honest about its heroes — all had great faults. All needed vision and faith. Sarah was one key person in God's plan for the world. But she needed to be strengthened. Genesis 18 tells us how God did it.

Abraham was sitting on his "front porch" one day when Jesus and two angels appeared. He immediately worshipped (Shachah = "bowed down") the Lord. This is the first usage of the Hebrew word "Shachah" in Scripture. Hospitable Abraham requested the three to stay while he had a calf killed and Sarah baked fresh bread.

The three visitors had two messages. The first message was that 90-year-old Sarah would have a son within a year. Eavesdropping from inside the tent, Sarah laughed in her heart as she thought about it. The Lord Jesus knows everything about everybody and He knew Sarah's heart response. He asked Abraham why Sarah laughed. She heard the question and, speaking through the tent, lied about it. The Lord knew she lied and called her on it. She must have no doubt about her role in God's plan.

Is your faith weak? Maybe you have trouble trusting God and He wants to strengthen you for a great purpose. He has ways to accomplish it! He knows every thought in your heart. He knows how to toughen your resolve. Let Him do His work in you.

ABRAHAM INTERCEDES

*Then the L*ORD *said, "Shall I hide from Abraham what I am about to do?"*

Genesis 18:17

FORMER WHEATON COLLEGE baseball player Todd Beamer became a hero when he and three other athletes interrupted the plans of terrorists aboard Flight 93 on September 11, 2001. He relied on Jesus Christ for strength and composure to respond quickly and wisely. We know he asked a GTE operator to recite The Lord's Prayer and Psalm 23 with him before saying, "Let's Roll," and leading the attack on the hijackers.

God isn't a terrorist. When He came down to investigate the wicked city of Sodom, the painful cry for help against the sinful wickedness of Sodom was very great. Sodom was known for homosexuality, but it was also destroyed because of its arrogance, gluttony, indifference to the poor, and pride (Ezekiel 16:49-50). The Sodomites had recently been miraculously delivered by God through Abraham and they had heard of Melchizedek.

Abraham had been very hospitable to his three visitors (Hebrews 13:2). As the Lord was about to leave for Sodom, Abraham walked with them. The LORD honored Abraham by revealing His plans. Why did God tell Abraham what He would do? The LORD had given the land to Abraham and his descendants and He wanted Abraham to know why some cities were to be destroyed. Secondly, Abraham was walking in close fellowship with God, and such people are given more insight (Hosea 14:9). Thirdly, Abraham must teach his children about God's holiness. His patience with man's sin has a limit. Fourthly, Abraham needed to know the reason for the approaching destruction of the cities. Abraham could have had a distorted view of God if the Lord hadn't explained what He was going to do. God did not have to "go down" to know about the great evil in Sodom. He is omniscient. He wanted Abraham to know that He knew the full situation before He acted in severe judgment.

Abraham was as worried for Lot as Todd Beamer was concerned for the White House and U.S. Capitol buildings. Unlike the terrorists, he knew God made distinctions between the wicked and the righteous. As the two angels headed for Sodom to fulfill their mission, Abraham approached the Lord, interceding for any righteous ones in Sodom. Hoping there were 50, he asked if they would be destroyed along with the ungodly. He appealed to God's justice. The Lord promised to spare the *entire* wicked city for the sake of 50 righteous ones! Then Abraham had a second thought. There may not be that many righteous people in Sodom! There may not be 45, 40, 30, 20, or even 10 believers in Sodom! God would have spared the whole city for the sake of 10 people, but they weren't there. Abraham probably thought of Lot's family. Lot was a believer in God, but he'd lost his influence for good! He couldn't even influence his own family. Yet, Lot was saved! God rescued him before He destroyed the ungodly with fire from heaven!

Notice several lessons from Genesis 18. God isn't eager to bring judgment upon any person or city. God reveals His secrets to those who walk with Him. Abraham knew what was going to happen to Sodom (Amos 3:7). Sudden destruction came upon the Sodomites. It doesn't take many prayers to prevail upon God for Him to act. Abraham prayed alone!

God spared righteous Lot and he would have spared the whole city for the sake of 10 righteous people. He would preserve the wicked for the sake of the righteous. The righteous just weren't there!

God didn't stop answering until Abraham stopped asking! What a great example of intercessory prayer.

LOT AND COMPROMISE

The two angels arrived at Sodom in the evening, and Lot was sitting in the gateway of the city.

Genesis 19:1

TOMMY DUNBAR was the Texas Rangers' first selection in the secondary phase of the 1981 draft. In 1985, he opened the season as a part-time starter. By late April, Tommy was hitting .417. In May, he tripped over first base and was put on the disabled list. He hit .161 the rest of the way and was sent to Class AAA Oklahoma City in July. His career faded so fast that he never appeared in another Rangers' game.

Lot was a righteous man who also started strong but faded fast. Though he was a terrible compromiser, we know he was declared righteous only because Peter said so in II Peter 2:8. Like Abraham, God declared Lot righteous not because of works, but because of faith (Genesis 15:6). But Lot's compromise cost him everything in this world. He was wealthy when he "pitched his tent near Sodom," one of the most wicked cities ever to disgrace the earth (Genesis 13:12). Sodom was one of five wicked cities, probably within three miles of each other near the southern end of the Dead Sea. Its name is now given to the vile practice of homosexuality, for which it was infamous. Before long, Lot had left his tents and moved into Sodom (14:12). Soon afterwards, Lot had a political position, evidently presiding over legal transactions at the city gate. He was probably accepted because of his wealth, but he was never happy in Sodom (II Peter 2:8). There is no evidence Lot ever told the Sodomites about the Living God. He had wealth and influence and he wanted the best of both worlds.

When the two destroying angels appeared as men, Lot knew it would be very dangerous for them to spend the night in the city square. He insisted they come to his house. Evidently, they were very handsome, for soon the homosexual men of Sodom surrounded Lot's house and demanded the visitors come out to be raped. The orgy would probably have resulted in their murder as well.

Lot protected his guests, but incredibly offered his two virgin daughters to the mob! Even if he knew the homosexual males would have no interest in his daughters, he had become a terrible father! His offer only made the "gays" more angry and he quickly learned he had no real friends in Sodom. The strong doors of that day had no outside latch, and Lot was rescued by the angels, who pulled him back inside, slammed the door, and struck the mob with blindness. The Sodomites were so hardened in sin that even this judgment did not cause them to repent.

Next, Lot hurried to warn his sons-in-law of the doom of Sodom. But he had no godly influence and they laughed at him. He was a failure as a father because of compromise with the world. The sons-in-law perished with everyone else when God rained sulfur and brimstone upon Sodom and the other cities of the once fertile plain. A catastrophic explosion was ignited over them.

God says homosexuality is a capital offense (Leviticus 18:22-30, 20:13). It seems to be the last stage of depravity before a society is destroyed, for it defiled the land around Sodom and Gomorrah (Leviticus 18:25; Jude 7). Yet, a punishment greater than physical destruction awaits those who reject the Lord Jesus Christ (Matthew 11:23-24). God rescued Lot — but he lost everything in the world because of his compromises.

THE CONSEQUENCES OF COMPROMISE

But Lot's wife looked back, and she became a pillar of salt.

Genesis 19:26

THE STANDARD MAJOR LEAGUE contract prohibits a player from a long list of career-threatening activities. These include skiing, skydiving, spelunking, motorcycle riding, and other professional sports. Players pay the consequences of compromise in these areas. In 1994, the Braves voided $4.6 million of Ron Gant's salary and released him when he crashed his dirt bike and broke his leg!

Lot also paid the consequences of compromise — he lost every worldly possession and his family — because of living in Sodom. Let's examine his story:

Sodom and the other cities were to be destroyed early in the morning, before anyone had left for work in the countryside and before any visitors came to town. But Lot, his wife, and their two daughters wouldn't stop compromising. The destroying angels had to pull them out of Sodom toward the safety of the mountains. When they begged to go to Zoar, God allowed it and spared Zoar. But Lot's wife, longing for her home in Sodom, looked back. She was immediately turned into a pillar of salt! Her heart remained in the culture of Sodom and it cost her everything. Today, when Arabs see one of the many salt pillars in the area, they call them, "Lot's wife." Jesus said, "Remember Lot's wife" as a warning to those who would cling to their earthly life and lose eternal life (Luke 17:32).

It was difficult to get Lot and his two daughters out of Sodom, but it was even more difficult to get Sodom out of Lot and his daughters! As the only survivors of Sodom, they were probably not well-received in evil Zoar, a nearby sister city. Soon, they fled to one of the many caves in the mountains. Possibly pride kept Lot from returning to Abraham.

Lot's story grew even more sordid. Unaccustomed to trusting God, Lot's daughters reasoned that incest was the only way they would ever have children and continue their family line. So, they got Lot drunk and slept with him on successive nights. From their sons came Moab ("from the father") and Benammi ("son of my people"), two nations which made frequent war on Israel. Eventually, these nations were integrated into the Arab peoples.

Moses recorded Lot's story as a lesson to Israel and to us. It's referred to often in other Scriptures. Did Israel learn from Lot? No! Years later, an almost identical event took place in Gibeah, a town of the tribe of Benjamin (Judges 19-20). The Israelites became just as evil as the pagans around them.

What about us? We must learn of God's hatred of sin and flee compromise with any form of it. What must God think of America today? What does He think of your personal compromise? May we not repeat the compromises of Lot, lest we suffer the consequences!

ABRAHAM'S BESETTING SIN

. . ..Abraham said of his wife Sarah, "She is my sister,"
then Abimelech King of Gerar sent for Sarah and took her.
Genesis 20:2

THE GIANTS' BENNY KAUFF repeated his baserunning mistake on May 26, 1916. Benny was so anxious to steal second base, he set a Major League record by being picked off first base three times in one game! The opposing pitcher was probably glad to see him get on first!

Abraham and Sarah repeated their mistakes, too. After all God had promised in His appearances to them and after several successes, they repeatedly stumbled in the area of integrity. This besetting sin had to be conquered before they could have Isaac and enjoy the blessings of God's promise fulfilled.

Wealthy Abraham moved again. But he was still afraid of being killed for his wife Sarah, who was even beautiful at age 86! He lived near the coast of Gerar, 12 miles south of Gaza. When he and Sarah lied to King Abimelech about their relationship, the King of Gerar took her away from Abraham! As punishment, God prevented anyone in Abimelech's household from conceiving children and He warned Abimelech in a dream of his impending death. God called Abraham a prophet. A prophet is one who reveals God's nature and purpose. God always takes it seriously when someone mistreats His prophets (Psalm 105:15).

Early the next morning, King Abimelech repented and returned Sarah. He also gave Abraham sheep, cattle, slaves, and money as compensation, and he allowed him to live anywhere he chose. This pagan King of Gerar feared Almighty God. He acted more righteously than Abraham acted!

God had a plan to preserve Abraham's marriage and ultimately bring the Messiah into the world through his descendants. But Abraham, the "father of faith," had to be rescued repeatedly from the effects of his half-truths. A half-truth presented as the full truth is an untruth! He had to stop this besetting sin before God would bless him.

Is there some sin that keeps God from blessing you? Until you confess and forsake it, the LORD will postpone His full blessing on your life. Abraham and Sarah waited a long time for God's blessing. How long do you want to wait? Would you like to confess your sin now?

Sibling Rivalry

But Sarah saw that the son whom Hagar the Egyptian had borne to Abraham was mocking, and she said to Abraham, "Get rid of that slave woman and her son, for that slave woman's son will never share in the inheritance with my son Isaac."

Genesis 21:9-10

RIVALRY HAS BECOME a part of sports, but some people take it to ridiculous levels. On August 28, 2000, two tee-ball coaches in Miami were suspended for their parts in a brawl involving nearly two dozen adults. These rivals had stormed the field to protest an umpire's call! Four-and five-year-old players watched as the adults "duked it out" over their tee-ball game! Thankfully, no one was seriously injured!

Sibling rivalry has played a major part in world history. It began with Cain and Abel and continued with Ishmael and Isaac. Let's examine their story.

On the day Isaac was ceremoniously weaned (two to three years old), Ishmael (now a teenager) mocked him. Ishmael probably resented the unusual attention being showered upon Isaac and he revealed his true nature. Sarah heard the taunts and insisted that Abraham get rid of both Ishmael and Hagar. It was impossible for the two to coexist peacefully in one household.

When God spoke to Abraham this time, He told him to listen to Sarah. It was through Isaac that Abraham's offspring would be "reckoned" and God's promises fulfilled (v 12). Though God promised Ishmael would survive to become a nation, Abraham was greatly distressed as he sent Hagar and Ishmael away.

Near death in the desert of Beersheba, Hagar and Ishmael were miraculously spared by God. He grew up, became a skilled archer, and fathered many of the Arabs, a people who became hostile toward all their brothers (Genesis 25:18).

In Galatians 4:22-31, Paul applied the story of Hagar and Ishmael to the principle that we can never mix law (old covenant) and grace (new covenant) as a means of salvation or daily living. To mix the two destroys both! Likewise, because the natural (Ishmael) is the enemy of the supernatural (Isaac), the natural means of living must be "put out." Natural ways of living and understanding never please God. We must make a conscious decision to "reckon" the flesh dead and to live in the spirit (Romans 6). This "sibling rivalry" is internal for the Christian, for the flesh always mocks the spirit! We can never live in harmony with both natures! To try to live both naturally and spiritually produces "spiritual schizophrenia."

TREATY OF A TRAVELER

So that place was called Beersheba, because the two men swore an oath there.

Genesis 21:31

JEFF KING WAS HAPPY in Pittsburgh. In December 1994, the Pirate third baseman took an 11-percent pay cut to stay in Pittsburgh instead of shopping for a better deal as a free agent. "Maybe I could find a better situation as a free agent, but why risk it when I'm perfectly happy where I am?" he asked. But the nature of pro sports is such that Jeff was later moved anyway. He concluded his career with some great seasons in Kansas City.

Abraham traveled throughout the Promised Land more than some Major League ball players switch teams. He temporarily settled in place after place. On more than one occasion, he paid for the land where he lived. He dug wells and built altars.

For a long time, Abraham lived at the southern edge of the Promised Land, 45 miles southwest of Jerusalem. Abraham named a well he had dug there "Beersheba," meaning "well of the oath," because of a treaty he made with those who lived nearby. This place later became a city.

Abimelech was leader of some traders living along the Mediterranean coast who became known as the Philistines. They would later oppress Israel, though their lapse into idolatry and superstition was gradual! Abimelech knew Abraham was blessed by God, was wealthy, and was deceptive, for he had lied twice about his wife's identity. So, he proposed a treaty to insure coexistence and grazing rights. Abraham used the occasion to protest the confiscation of his well. In open grazing land, the digging of a well signified ownership. By this treaty, Abraham obtained legal right to dwell in the area.

The account of this treaty, recorded by Moses as Israel began to enter the Promised Land years later, assured Israel of legal ownership. They had orders from God to possess what was already their land. They had every reason to enter the land God promised to them.

THE SUPREME TEST

Abraham answered, "God himself will provide the lamb for the burnt offering, my son." And the two of them went on together.

Genesis 22:8

BASEBALL IS A GAME of tough tests. A pitcher who throws 98 mph severely tests hitters in the late innings of a close game. Overcoming injury through rehab taxes a person's will to return to the lineup. The long, grueling travel schedule with 162 games is an exhausting test for everyday players.

No test in athletics can match the supreme test God gave to Abraham. His earlier tests (leaving family, moving far from home, disinheriting Ishmael and sending him away) were preliminary to the big one. Contrary to what Abraham knew of God and to his own logic, Abraham was told to go to Mt. Moriah and sacrifice Isaac as a burnt offering! No reason was given. Yet, the order was clear.

Isaac ("laughter") was a joy to both Abraham and Sarah. As the son of God's promise, he had been worth waiting for. He was probably 30 to 33 years old and the only son of God's promise. He was Abraham's *only* legitimate son in the legal sense. Ishmael never enjoyed the rights of Isaac. The term "only begotten" (KJV) refers to status as a unique son. God knew Abraham loved Isaac. This is the first use of the word "love" in Scripture and this love of a father for a son is the foundation of all other types of love! What a picture of God the Father and Jesus, His Son!

God was testing (not tempting) Abraham and he often tests us (James 1:2, I Peter 1:6-7). Abraham probably never told Sarah, but he obeyed immediately. He fully intended to sacrifice his only son from the day he set out on the three-day, 50-mile journey.

Abraham and Isaac traveled to the mountain area where Solomon would later build the Temple and Jesus would die still later for our sins, Near his destination, Abraham dismissed his servants and said, "We'll worship ("recognize, acknowledge, and bow down to God") and then we'll come back to you." This is the first use of the word "worship" in Scripture. Abraham had confidence that God would raise Isaac from the dead (Hebrews 11:19). He sadly continued up the hill, feeling how God himself felt 2,000 years later as He gave His only begotten Son for the sins of mankind. When Isaac asked where the sacrifice was, Abraham said, "God will provide the lamb." He spoke prophetically of Jesus, the Lamb of God (John 1:29), though he didn't know the details! He passed God's supreme test.

Isaac had the faith of his father. He was willing to lay down his life in obedience, for he could easily have escaped. What a picture of Jesus Christ!

God stopped Abraham just before he killed Isaac, for Abraham proved he feared ("reverenced, trusted, obeyed") God. He was justified by faith, but his work of offering Isaac proved his faith was genuine (James 2:20-24). The Lord provided a ram (another representation of Jesus) to replace Isaac. Abraham joyfully untied Isaac and killed the ram in his place! He learned much about God that day, and he called the area Jehovah-Jirah ("The Lord will Provide").

God spared Abraham's son, but not His own Son (Romans 8:32). He promised to bless all nations through Jesus Christ, the "seed" of Abraham (Galatians 3:16). The Lord Jesus Christ died willingly for the sins of the lost people of earth. Nothing in all of history compares to His ultimate sacrifice!

SARAH'S DEATH IN CANAAN

Afterward Abraham buried his wife Sarah in the cave in the field of Machpelah near Mamre (which is at Hebron) in the land of Canaan.

Genesis 23:19

JACK BUCK was an institution in St. Louis. The 77-year-old broadcaster who began calling Cardinals games on the radio in 1954, died on June 18, 2002. As Diamondbacks manager Bob Brenly said, "He was baseball for a lot of people who grew up in the Midwest." The Cardinals wore black patches on their uniforms after his death and stenciled his initials on the grass in his memory.

Abraham must have been away from home when Sarah died suddenly (v 2). Evidently, they had moved from Beersheba back to Hebron, 20 miles south of the future city of Jerusalem. Sarah was a godly woman who submitted to Abraham (I Peter 3:5-6). As such, she is an example to Christian women. She was 137 years old when she died in 2028 bc.

Abraham grieved for his wife. As a constant traveler in Canaan (Hebrews 11:9), he needed a burial site in the land of God's promise. He offered to buy land from Ephron, a Hittite, who owned it. Ephron offered to give the site, but Abraham didn't want to be indebted to an unbeliever. So, he obtained legal ownership at a steep price, completing the transaction in the presence of legal witnesses in one of the first sales of property on record.

Sarah's burial in Canaan testified, both to the conquering Israeli people of Moses' day and to the Canaanites, that the land was home to Abraham. The cave of her burial became the graves of Abraham, Isaac, Rebekah, Leah, and Jacob. Though the Hittites were destroyed in 1200 bc, an important Moslem mosque today stands on the location. Yet, because Isaac (not Ishmael) is the child of promise, the land belongs to Israel!

Read Genesis 24 and 22:20-24

A WIFE FOR ISAAC

And my master made me swear an oath, and said, 'You must not get a wife for my son from the daughters of the Canaanites, in whose land I live, but go to my father's family and to my own clan, and get a wife for my son.'

Genesis 24:37-38

ONE FACTOR IN DRAFTING a player is his signability. Every pro team recognizes talent, but if a player won't sign a contract because he wants too much money or he wants to finish school, it's not wise to waste a draft pick on him. Teams must do their homework to determine signability before they draft!

Abraham faced a daunting challenge as he considered the "signability" of a wife for his son. To produce a great nation, Isaac must have a Godly wife! A Godly wife was not to be found among the unbelieving pagans of Canaan and there could be no compromise in her selection.

Though Abraham had probably not seen his brother Nahor for 60 years, he knew Nahor had respect for the Lord. News flowed back and forth from Nahor in Haran to Abraham in Canaan and Abraham knew of children born in Haran (22:20-24). Abraham knew Isaac must not leave Canaan, the land God promised to give him (vs 6, 8). If he left, the temptation to stay in Haran might be too great. So, he directed his chief servant, a loyal and reliable man, to travel the 400 miles to Haran to find a wife for 40-year-old Isaac. According to custom, the servant vowed faithfulness by placing his hand under Abraham's thigh, agreeing that if he was not faithful that Abraham's offspring could avenge his unfaithfulness.

Taking 10 camels and loaded with gifts, the servant traveled to Haran. Outside the town of Nahor, he waited and prayed for specific guidance. He asked that the girl who would give both him and his camels water at the

75

evening water gathering would be God's choice for Isaac. God answered his prayer before he finished praying (vs 15, 45)! Rebekah was kind, beautiful and pure (v 16). She watered 10 guzzling camels, each of which can drink up to 25 gallons! The servant presented her with expensive jewelry and she ran home with news of the stranger and his camels. When Rebekah's brother (Laban) heard of the wealthy servant of legendary Abraham, he welcomed him into their house. After hearing his story, they agreed to let Rebekah go, accepted costly gifts to seal the marriage contract, and housed the servant overnight. In the morning, the devious Laban tried to postpone her departure, but Rebekah agreed to go without delay. She returned with the servant to meet Isaac in southern Palestine, 25 miles northwest of Kadesh-Barnea. Rebekah became Isaac's wife and was a great comfort to him.

The entire event was orchestrated by God (vs 7, 21, 40). He led Rebekah to Isaac one step at a time (Proverbs 3:5-6). The event pictures God the Father (Abraham) sending the servant (Holy Spirit) to obtain a wife (all who believe) for His Son, Jesus Christ!

God's "draft pick" for Isaac was immediately "signed" and no marriage was more vital in world history! If God would bless all nations through Abraham's offspring, Isaac needed a Godly wife. Isaac trusted his father's judgment. God led the servant to Rebekah, who was raised to trust God. She was a virgin who was willing to leave home without delay to marry Isaac. God gave the best to Isaac, who left the choice to Him!

Isaac — the Sole Heir

Abraham left everything he owned to Isaac.

Genesis 25:5

AMONG THE 62 SPORTSWRITERS AND BROADCASTERS who voted in the 1992 AP poll, Corky Simpson stood alone for the entire 17 weeks. He voted Alabama #1. Irate fans flooded him with hate mail and columnists ridiculed his opinion. One Florida woman called him "morally irresponsible and inherently evil." But Corky was proved right. The Tide won the national championship by dominating Miami 34-13 in the Sugar Bowl.

Isaac's selection as heir of God's promise was as unpopular as Corky's choice of Alabama. But it was just as right, for God was the One who chose him! The story is remarkable even after God gave Abraham the ability to father Isaac at age 100! Abraham eventually married Keturah, through whom he fathered six more sons. All these children came from a man whose body was as good as dead (Hebrews 11:12)! I Chronicles 1:32 calls Keturah his "concubine." God's Word records sins it doesn't approve, though Abraham could have married his concubine after Sarah died. Her six sons were the origin of several Arab tribes east of Palestine. Ishmael's 12 sons began more Arab tribes (Genesis 17:20) and they lived in much conflict among themselves. Lot's sons began still more Arab nations.

Abraham was indeed the "father of many nations" (Genesis 17:6). He gave gifts to all his children, but his estate and the promises of God belonged to Isaac. Isaac's son, Jacob, had his name changed to "Israel." History reveals great jealousy of Israel on the part of the Arabs, but God sovereignly gave the land of Palestine to Israel.

God has never changed His plan to bless the world through Israel. Israelites will be blessed as a nation when they are in the land of Palestine worshipping the Messiah, Jesus Christ. They were told to never mistreat the Arabs (Exodus 22:21) and to give aliens an inheritance, too (Ezekiel 47:21-22).

Abraham died at age 175 and he was "gathered to his people." Jesus called this place "Abraham's bosom" (Luke 16:22). Clearly, there is a resurrection and the Old Testament taught it. Isaac and Ishmael renewed acquaintances at Abraham's funeral. That must have been some sight! Isaac, with his servants, was in contact with Ishmael and his armed followers. At the funeral, they had peace. But it was a peace that wouldn't last.

RIVALRY REVISITED

Isaac, who had a taste for wild game, loved Esau, but Rebekah loved Jacob.

Genesis 25:28

NO RIVALRY IS MORE STORIED than Nebraska vv. Oklahoma in football. Every time the teams play when they are highly ranked, references are made to the 1971 "Game of the Century," won by Nebraska, 35-31.

"At (age) 21, I knew it was an important game but I never thought that we'd be talking about it (nearly) 30 years later," said OU quarterback Jack Mildren.

Rivalry between twin boys is a bit unusual. They always seem to have much in common. But Jacob and Esau were not typical. They were very different in temperament and appearance. Their births weren't even typical. Their mother, Rebekah, was barren after 20 years of marriage. Then Isaac prayed for her and she conceived twins! God had already determined Isaac and Rebekah would have children, but He seems to delight in our prayers and Isaac did much better than his father Abraham had done in the same situation!

The twins fought inside the womb and struggling Rebekah prayed again. She asked God, "Why is this happening to me?" God answered, revealing that two boys, representing two nations in conflict, were inside her. The elder was decreed by God to serve the younger.

Esau was born first. He was red and hairy and he became a hunter. Jacob was born holding onto Esau's heel. He was a deceiver and a mama's boy. Unwisely, Isaac and Rebekah chose favorites.

One day Esau was very hungry after a hunting trip. Evidently he had shot nothing to eat. Jacob was cooking stew. Esau wanted some immediately and Jacob saw his chance. He desired to obtain Esau's rights as firstborn.

These rights included twice the possessions of other heirs, authority, and responsibility to transmit the word and ways of God. Possibly Jacob made the demand in jest and was surprised the Godless Esau accepted. Maybe he made the demand in disgust with Esau's indifference to anything spiritual. Regardless, Esau didn't want any spiritual leadership and wouldn't have lead spiritually anyway. He wasn't starving, but his lifestyle put him in constant danger. He legally swapped his inheritance for a bowl of stew! Hebrews 12:16-17 says he later desired the benefits of the firstborn, but he had permanently lost them.

Contrary to custom, younger Jacob was God's choice before birth for greater blessing (Romans 9:10-13). But he was wrong to deceptively obtain the birthright from his brother. He schemed to get what God had already promised and his sin alienated his father and brother.

Esau begat the Edomites, who served Israel (Jacob) until they revolted in David's day (II Chronicles 21:8). Obediah pronounced their doom.

Do you value spiritual things? Or, like Esau, do you avoid God and His purposes?

Do you wait confidently upon God? Or, like Jacob, do you scheme and plot how to get ahead? Both attitudes are wrong, and both carry consequences.

LIKE FATHER, LIKE SON

When the men of that place asked him about his wife, he said, "She is my sister, because he was afraid to say, she is my wife." He thought, "The men of this place might kill me on account of Rebekah, because she is beautiful."

Genesis 26:7

HARRY CAREY WAS RARELY HOME on summer evenings, but he never missed his son's bedtime. As Skip listened to his father's Cardinal broadcasts, every night at 8:30 Harry would say, "Timeout for station identification. Good night, Skip. This is the Cardinal Baseball Network."

Skip became a broadcaster and has announced 27 years of Braves' games. Furthermore, his son, Chip, is now a Cubs broadcaster on WGN. The three worked a game together only once, in 1991. Like father, like son, and like grandson!

Like the Careys, Abraham, Isaac, and Jacob lived similar lives and experienced similar trials. Isaac for example, went through some of the same trials as his father Abraham. He overcame some of these trials and he failed in others. Genesis 26 records a failure.

A rare famine occurred in the land of promise and, like his father, Isaac was on the move. He went to Gerar, an area toward the coast and on the way to Egypt. But God didn't want Isaac in Egypt. The Lord appeared to him and told him to stay in Gerar. To his credit, Isaac obeyed. Evidently, this was the first time the Lord had appeared to Isaac since the Mt. Moriah incident some 50 years earlier.

Pagan Philistines lived in Gerar, though most still lived on Crete, from which they would come in great numbers centuries later. Like Abraham, Isaac had a fear of man. He feared for his life because Rebekah was still beautiful and he could be killed for her. Like Abraham, he lied by telling the Philistines she was his sister. Abraham had done the same thing! Abraham's lie was a half-truth, but Isaac told a total lie. There is no generation gap concerning sin! What we do in moderation, our children will take a step further!

One day, Abimelech (a title) saw Isaac and Rebekah behaving only as husband and wife should behave. He was caressing her. Abimelech realized Isaac had deceived his people concerning Rebekah and he called him to account. This Abimelech was not the same Philistine leader of Abraham's day, but he must have known of God's judgment upon his tribe when Sarah was taken from Abraham. He was appalled at Isaac's lie and he was afraid of what Almighty God might do to anyone who would take Rebekah from Isaac! So, he issued the death penalty for anyone who would molest God's chosen ones!

All God's people go through many tests to refine their character. I Peter 1:7 says, "These have come so that your faith — of greater worth than gold, which perishes even though refined by fire — may be proved genuine and may result in praise, glory and honor when Jesus Christ is revealed." We must overcome trials without sin, for the glory of God and for our children's sake. If Abraham had overcome his fear of man, Isaac would have had a Godly example to follow when he faced the same trial! But he failed, as did Isaac. Like father, like son!

WATER WELLS AND ENEMIES

He moved on from there and dug another well, and no one quarreled over it. He named it Rehoboth, saying, "Now the LORD has given us room and we'll flourish in the land."
Genesis 26:22

THE CONFLICT OVER WHO OWNED Barry Bonds 73rd home-run ball of 2001 seemed to go on and on. Alex Popov caught the ball, but after fans mobbed him in the bleachers, Patrick Hayashi ended up with it. It was a year and a day before a judge ruled they had to split the estimated $1 million it would generate. When the ball was finally sold for far less money and legal fees paid, it became doubtful whether either man retained much money!

Conflict seemed to go on and on for Isaac. He became a farmer during a famine, and God blessed him so much that the Philistines envied him. When they plugged his water wells, he moved away to avoid armed conflict, even though he was the more powerful (v. 16). He dug more wells, the enemy contested them, and he moved again until they left him alone. He showed great patience and restraint when mistreated.

Finally, Isaac moved to Beersheba, where he had lived with his father Abraham after the Mt. Moriah experience. It was in Beersheba that the LORD appeared to him again. God reassured Isaac of His blessing on his descendants. His Philistine enemies recognized that Isaac had the help of Almighty God. They became uneasy and requested that he sign a peace treaty, since he was more powerful! Isaac's patience and God's blessing led to peace in this case. He showed no bitterness or desire to retaliate.

Just as the Philistines attacked Isaac's water sources, the enemy of our souls (Satan) always attacks the source of our strength: the Word of God. When he sees us prospering, he tries to stop the flow of God's Word into our lives. He hinders preachers, tells us we're too busy to study God's Word daily, and casts doubt on the truth of Scripture and its relevance for life. He uses envy, even among church members, to hinder anyone who studies God's Word. Satan doesn't care about religious activity or civic events, but he hates the water of God's Word as it satisfies our thirsty souls!

Keep digging until the well of living water surfaces! Find a pastor who believes and faithfully preaches God's Word. Meditate day and night upon His Word (Psalm 1) and God promises blessing and peace in your life!

ONE DECEPTIVE FAMILY

Esau said, "Isn't he rightly named Jacob? He has de-ceived me these two times: He took my birthright, and now he's taken my blessing!"

Genesis 27:36

THE HIDDEN BALL TRICK is an act of deceit that has been around baseball since the game began. In the first year of the National League, on May 25, 1876, Cap Anson of the Chicago White Stockings was caught off third when Hartford shortstop Tom "Scoops" Carey concealed the ball between pitches. Bill Deane of the Society for American Baseball Research has counted 140 successful attempts since, most recently by the Giants against the Dodgers on June 26, 1999.

The family God chose through which to fulfill His prom-ises greatly complicated its existence through deceit. It's a good thing the promises depended upon God's sovereignty and not upon man's dependability! Let's look at the devi-ous story in Genesis 27.

One hundred thirty-seven-year-old Isaac was blind and he believed he was near death (he would live to be 180, however). For some reason, the introspective and nonagressive old man favored his rough-and-tumble old-est son, Esau. Isaac sent Esau to kill a deer, bring the venison, and prepare a private meal for the two of them. He intended to pass on his material, political, military, and spiritual inheritance to 77-year-old Esau, even though he knew God had said that Esau's twin brother was to inherit these blessings! Favoritism and disobedience were about to tear this family apart.

Rebekah was eavesdropping, stealing a conversation not intended for her. She developed a devious plan to trick Isaac into blessing Jacob, the younger twin whom she fa-vored. She naively thought God's plan depended upon the formal decree of Isaac. But God had already given His blessing to Jacob and deceit was unnecessary.

Jacob pursued the scheme. It was a tense situation, with no time to waste before Esau returned from the hunt. Jacob lied twice when blind Isaac asked him point-blank about his identity. He even brought God into his deception (v. 20). Though God did not approve, the Scripture records the events as they took place. Jacob was successful in stealing what God had given him anyway, but his deception cost him dearly. He would enjoy very little peace for a long time.

Esau returned and was furious that his mother and brother had tricked his father and stolen what he considered his blessing. Carnal and profane (he had married two pagan women), Esau was not interested in spiritual leadership and responsibility. He desired the material and political advantages of the inheritance. He sought his father's blessing with tears (Hebrews 12:16-17), but it was too late. His life of immorality and indifference to God had caught up with him. The only prophecy for his offspring (Edomites) was one of violence, servitude and successful rebellion against Jacob (Israel). Maybe this partly satisfied his bitterness and frustration.

In this incident, every member of Isaac's family lacked faith! No one knows what would have happened if Isaac had blessed Esau. Perhaps God would have killed them both on the spot! Though God did not approve of the deception, partiality, or disobedience of this family, His plan remained to bless the world through them!

CONSEQUENCES

*Then Isaac sent Jacob on his way, and he went to
Paddan Aram, to Laban . . .*

Genesis 28:5

FISHING TOURNAMENTS PAY OFF in big money for big
catches. But deceit always brings about undesirable consequences for the deceivers. At the 2002 Great Ontario
Salmon Derby in Canada, local angler Gary Morrison al-
legedly rammed 7F(1,2) pounds of lead pipe, rocks, and sink-
ers into a Chinook he claimed to have caught. He faced up
to eight years in jail for this and another fraud.

The deceit in Isaac's dysfunctional family also bore
much undesirable fruit. But what else could be expected?
Sin always brings with it the consequences of estranged
relationships.

Esau became vindictive and neurotic, vowing to kill
his twin brother when their father died. He probably had
no respect for his mother because of her deception.

Rebekah feared for Jacob's life. Not telling Isaac of
Esau's anger, she used Esau's marriages to two godless
women (26:34-35) as an excuse to get Isaac to send Jacob
to Haran for a wife, thereby saving him from being slain.
She intended that Jacob only be gone until Esau's anger
cooled, but a few days became 20 years and she died in
the meantime. Rebekah never saw her favorite son again.

Isaac realized that God was blessing Jacob with the
promises given to Abraham. He went along with Rebekah's
plan because the marriage of those who know God with
those who are godless is disastrous. He had obtained his
own wife from Abraham's family in Haran, so he encouraged Jacob to obtain a wife from the same people, where
the deceiver (Jacob) will get a lesson from a bigger deceiver (Laban)!

Esau wanted to please Isaac, but he had no spiritual

insight. Knowing Isaac was upset with his pagan wives, Esau married a daughter of Ishmael. But the Ishmaelites were no more in the Godly line than were the Philistines, Canaanites, or Hittites!

It seemed Isaac's family couldn't win for losing. When their eyes left the Lord and His Word, each made foolish decisions that bore undesirable consequences. The same is true for us. Our hope rests upon God and obedience to His Word. Our own ideas never bring peace and usually have consequences we don't like.

Jacob's Dream

He had a dream in which he saw a stairway resting on the earth, with its top reaching to heaven, and the angels of God were ascending and descending on it.

Genesis 28:12

IN 2002, JAKE PORTER had a dream fulfilled. As a senior at Northwest High School (Ohio), Jake came to practice every day and dressed for every game. Jake has inherited mental retardation. He never played a down until his coach, Dave Frantz, and the opposing coach, Derek DeWitt, called time-out, met at mid-field, and talked to their teams with DeWitt's Waverly High School team leading 42-0 and time running out. At DeWitt's suggestion, when play resumed 21 players parted ways. The ball was given to Jake, who was pointed toward the end zone. Twelve seconds later, he scored a touchdown in a dream come true! People left the bleachers in tears.

Jacob was alone, running away from Esau and heading to Paddan-Aram (Syria) to find a wife, when he had the dream of his life. He was probably scared and lonely. As far as we know, it was his first night away from home. Not by chance, he camped at a certain spot over 40 miles from his home. God was leading him, but he probably didn't realize it at the time (Jeremiah 10:23).

Using one of the many stones in the area for a pillow, he collapsed into a deep sleep. God revealed Himself to Jacob in a dream, demonstrating by angels going up and down on a stairway to heaven that He is interested and involved in the affairs of people on earth (Hebrews 1:14, 12:22; Psalm 103:29). God promised to give Jacob land, offspring, and blessing. This is the first of God's eight appearances to Jacob. He now had a personal relationship with the God of the universe!

Jacob's outlook changed. He now knew God was with him and he would return to Canaan, though he couldn't have known how long it would take to obtain a wife. He knew the land belonged to him and his offspring. Immediately, Jacob made a memorial out of his pillow! The site would be called Bethel ("House of God"). It was located six miles north of what later became Jerusalem.

Jacob now had a faith of his own. He had spent decades tied to his dominant mother's apron strings, under a weak father, and around a worldly brother. He would no longer depend upon the faith of his parents or upon his own deceptive ways. God was going to change him, just as He works in the lives of all His children! The standing stones he erected became sites of remembrance for future generations. They taught others about God (Joshua 4:6). Jacob promised God a tenth of all the Lord would give him. One day, he returned and built an altar at Bethel (Genesis 35:3, 7).

Years later, the Lord Jesus Christ was speaking to a Godly Israelite named Nathaniel (John 1:51). He claimed to be the stairway to Heaven! He is God and the only way to get to God. Jacob experienced Him personally. Have you?

WHAT GOES AROUND, COMES AROUND!

When morning came, there was Leah! So Jacob said to Laban, "What is this you have done to me? I served you for Rachel, didn't I? Why have you deceived me?"
Genesis 29:25

JOHN McENROE WAS A TENNIS STAR who had a severe anger problem. After retirement, he wrote, "I really was pretty much of a jerk." His anger was part of an act on the court, but it hurt him deeply in his life. In his autobiography, McEnroe wrote of faking anger on changeovers so he could put his face in a towel and cry over his crumbling marriage. He told of using marijuana to cope with life. He suffered greatly from his anger and deceit.

Deceitful Jacob suffered when he was on the receiving end of deceit. God is always working in the lives of His children and He used uncle Laban to discipline and grow Jacob. No one has ever reaped what he sowed quite as severely as Jacob (Galatians 6:7). Here's the story:

Jacob traveled almost 400 miles and approached Haran when he met some shepherds at a well who "just happened" to know his uncle Laban. Laban's daughter Rachel "just happened" to be on her way to water sheep (v. 6). A sovereign God is at work!

Jacob arrived with nothing and already he started giving orders to the shepherds. He wanted to meet Rachel privately and he was used to manipulating events during his first 77 years! After he watered her sheep, Jacob kissed her. This was a common greeting for a relative and he certainly relished it in this case! Rachel ran to tell her father, Laban, who welcomed Jacob to stay with him. Traditionally, a stranger was housed for three days, after which he was to state his name and his mission. Jacob was a hard worker, and he worked for an entire month. But uncle Laban was even more devious than Jacob! He probably saw Jacob and Rachel making eyes at each other and knew he couldn't stop the inevitable. When he asked Jacob what wages he wanted, all Jacob requested was Rachel. He agreed to work seven years for her!

After seven years, the marriage ceremony was performed! But slick Laban pulled a fast one. Custom dictated that the heavily veiled bride enter the groom's tent on the wedding night. It was just after a feast, and Jacob may have had too much to drink, so when Laban substituted the older Leah for the beautiful Rachel, Jacob was tricked. He thought he was having sex with Rachel! No one knows where Rachel was, but maybe she was forcibly detained by Laban's men!

When Jacob awoke in the morning and saw the unattractive Leah, he must have realized the payback for his own deceit. He now knew how his twin brother Esau felt. The deceiver had been deceived! He had trusted the wrong person (Laban) and had made a lifetime decision when he was not spiritually strong. He had married the wrong woman! But Laban wasn't done yet. He got Jacob to work seven more years in exchange for Rachel. Of course, that gave Jacob two wives, which was *not* God's will. All cases of multiple wives are a failure to follow God's plan and result in rivalry, jealousy, and strife. Such bad choices happen when people are at a spiritual low, and Jacob was at such a point. Yet, he was tragically making lifetime decisions and he couldn't resist Rachel. He got her after a week of sleeping with Leah. Each wife was given a servant girl. Altogether, Jacob endured 20 years of servitude to Laban. He served 14 years for his wives, and six years for cattle (31:41). God was developing his character, but the lessons must have been as hard as Jacob's head!

How is God developing your character? Do the events of your life seem unfair? Are you reaping what you have sown? Remember, God is a sovereign God who works in all things for His glory and your good.

LEAH'S CONSOLATION

When the Lord saw that Leah was not loved, he opened her womb, but Rachel was barren.

Genesis 29:31

"THREE FINGER" BROWN was enshrined in the Hall of Fame in 1949. He played for 14 years in the Major Leagues. Between 1902-1911, Brown averaged 30 victories per year. When Brown was seven years old, he lost his forefinger and part of his little finger and mangled the middle finger on his right hand in a corn-grinding accident. His consolation was that the damaged fingers imparted a sharper break to his curve ball. Ty Cobb said that Brown's curve ball was the most devastating pitch he ever faced.

Leah had been part of a terrible deception, but she loved Jacob. Jacob loved her sister Rachel and preferred to live with her. Leah must have been deeply hurt. But God saw her pain and gave her the consolation of six sons and one daughter. Leah kept trying to get Jacob to love and honor her because of childbearing. On one occasion, she even paid Rachel with mandrakes (a fruit believed by Orientals to aid conception) to get Jacob back into her bed. She hungered for affection and approval. She craved recognition and love. She seems to have honored God by their names and by giving Him credit for their births. If Jacob never saw her agony, God did.

Rachel became jealous of Leah and demanded children from Jacob. She gave her servant girl Bilhah to Jacob to produce a child for her household. A "pregnancy war" ensued! Twelve sons and a daughter were born as a result of Jacob's polygamy (two wives plus two servant girls who became wives). God's plan was one wife per man (Genesis 2:24). These 12 sons became the 12 tribes of Israel. The jealousy and strife of their mothers explains much of their tribal rivalry as they looked back to their origin. Later, Jacob had other daughters (37:35, 46:7–15).

God is so kind. He saw Leah's rejection and gave her children, including Judah, who became the tribe from which the King would come and Levi, the tribe of the Israeli priesthood. He is the God of great consolation for those who suffer. Leah discovered just how much He hears and helps!

Blessing Under a Tough Boss

In this way the man grew exceedingly prosperous and came to own large flocks, and maidservants and manservants, and camels and donkeys.

Genesis 30:43

THOUGH THE 1964 YANKEES suffered crippling injuries, first-year manager Yogi Berra led them to the World Series. They lost the Series to the Cardinals in seven games. How was Yogi rewarded? His boss fired him and hired Cardinals' manager Johnny Keane. Keane promptly led New York to where they hadn't been in 40 years: sixth place in 1965!

God can bless Yogi Berra or whomever He wants with prosperity. He can even bless hired workers like Jacob, who worked for a scheming, dishonest boss like Laban. When Jacob desired to return to his homeland in Canaan, selfish Laban deceived him into staying, for he knew (by pagan divination) that the Lord was blessing him because of Jacob! Crafty uncle Laban didn't intend to let Jacob leave with anything, but he told Jacob to name his wages anyway.

Jacob proposed that he keep the speckled, spotted, and streaked animals born into Laban's flocks. He put his inheritance in God's hands, for these animals were somewhat rare. Laban agreed to the plan, but quickly took several of these animals out of his flocks and sent them 12 miles away to his sons. This action severely reduced Jacob's wages.

Jacob, however, knew about breeding sheep. He was almost as crafty as his dishonest uncle. Either there was a stimulant inside the tree branches which induced sheep to mate at a higher rate, or the ruse of using stripped branches in water concealed his selective breeding techniques. Regardless, he grew wealthy in six years. God over-

95

ruled to the extent that the sheep bred in his favor. Large numbers of speckled or spotted animals were born (31:9-12). Two deceitful rich men were outgrowing the area!

Are you faithful to your boss, even if he is as deceitful as Laban? God wants us to be dependable workers. He can bless us in every circumstance and He will honor those who honor Him!

ESCAPE FROM LABAN

*Then the Lord said to Jacob, "Go back to the land of
your fathers and to your relatives, and I will be with you."*
Genesis 31:3

THE CINCINNATI REDS had the Dodgers' Davy Lopez
caught in a rundown on August 10, 1977. But after six
throws involving every Reds infielder, Lopes escaped! He
reached second base and scored on a single for the only
run of the game.

After Jacob had served Laban 14 years, he intended to
escape and go home. But God kept him in Paddan Aram
for six more years. Then the circumstances changed. The
attitudes of Laban, a Syrian, and his sons shifted against
Jacob as they saw God blessing Jacob and diminishing
Laban. The sons probably saw their inheritance slipping
away! Laban had cheated Jacob 10 times by changing his
wages, but no matter what he did, God prospered, protected, and promoted Jacob! Jacob's prosperity was entirely due to God's intervention and he knew it, for God
revealed it to him in a dream!

God instructed Jacob to return to the land of Canaan
(vv. 3, 13). Almighty God certainly did not want Jacob's
sons to grow up around Laban's increasingly pagan household. The Lord revealed Himself as the God of Bethel, where
Jacob first met Him and came to personally know Him.
How encouraging this must have been!

Jacob consulted privately with his wives. It would be
easier if both of Laban's daughters agreed with the move.
They did. This was another confirmation of God's will.
Laban's selfishness and deceit had caused even his own
daughters to lose respect for him (vv. 14-16). Both loved
Jacob, for he had served 14 years for them. Laban had
given them no financial security.

Before they left, Rachel stole her father's household idols (deceit runs in this family!). These clay or silver images may have implied rights to Laban's inheritance. Or, they may have been worshipped. Some think they were clay models of ancestors Shem and Noah. In any case, Laban was losing everything important to him. For her part, Rachel may have thought the images were "lucky." But one sin led to another, and later she lied to her father to cover her theft.

After three days, Laban heard about Jacob's escape. He took his sons and set out in hot pursuit. They probably intended to kill Jacob and take his herds of sheep and cattle. The night they caught up with Jacob's "trail drive," they set up camp, probably to prepare for combat the next day. But God appeared to Laban in a dream and warned him not to rebuke Jacob!

It must have been tense when a frustrated, bitter, and angry Laban rode into Jacob's camp the next day. He faked sadness over not being able to give Jacob's group a going-away party, but everyone saw through his lies. Finally, he made mild-mannered Jacob angry. Jacob released his pent-up emotions of 20 years. Unable to find his gods, Laban gave up the chase. The two deceivers made a stone heap to serve as a pillar of remembrance. It reminded them to quit cheating each other and served as a border between them.

Laban, the self-seeking hypocrite, was finally out of Jacob's life. Like many semi-spiritual businessmen today, he was self-serving and covetous. McGee says that Jacob graduated from Laban's "school of hard knocks." He had refused submission to God at home, so God put him under uncle Laban. He had deceived his own father (Isaac), and his father-in-law deceived him! Later, his own sons would deceive him about Joseph's death. Surely, Jacob reaped what he sowed!

CRISIS

Save me, I pray, from the hand of my brother Esau, for I am afraid he will come and attack me, and also the mothers with their children.

Genesis 32:11

LPGA PRO TERRY-JO MYERS is no stranger to crises. At age 21, she was stricken with a rare and painful bladder disease. She lived in constant and severe pain. When she resumed her career with the help of medication, she suffered two serious back injuries which required surgeries. Terry-Jo admits she can't handle her problems alone. "You're not ever supposed to get to where you don't need Him," she says.

Jacob was nearing a crisis. It was a crisis he couldn't handle on his own. Though he had been a poor example of a man of God, he was still God's man. God grew him by showing how powerless he was when he relied upon himself. The only way Jacob could produce any lasting "fruit" was to rely totally upon God.

God sent a troop of angels to meet Jacob on his way to Canaan, just as he had seen angels in his dream 20 years earlier when he left Canaan. He must have been greatly encouraged, for he named the site "Two Camps." He had a host of angels protecting him from Laban behind and a host protecting him from Esau ahead!

Jacob sent messengers to his twin brother Esau, from whom he had fled 20 years earlier. Providentially, Esau had moved south of Canaan. God had already prepared a place for Jacob! Esau's response was to bring 400 men toward Jacob's camp! Jacob was terrified. He was outgunned. He divided his trail drive into two groups, hoping one would survive the attack. Then he prayed the most fervent prayer of his life. Jacob finally got serious with

God and confessed his unworthiness. He acknowledged he did not deserve what He had been given. He prayed in harmony with God's Word and he called upon God to fulfill His promise. Jacob's prayer was powerful and effective.

Still, Jacob worried. Thinking he could pacify Esau, he sent over 550 goats, sheep, camels, cows, and donkeys as gifts to the advancing Esau. His brother would arrive the next day. If he was still angry, the slaughter would be over quickly.

Read Genesis 32:22-32

GOD PICKS A FIGHT

*So Jacob was left alone, and a man wrestled with him
until daybreak.*

Genesis 32:24

A FAN PICKED A FIGHT with a Houston player during a
1999 baseball game in Milwaukee. Right fielder Bill Spiers was attacked in the sixth inning when a lone assailant
ran onto the field, jumped him from behind, and knocked
him to the ground. Spiers suffered a whiplash before the
entire Astros bench and bullpen ran to his defense! The
attacker was handcuffed and led away by sheriff's deputies.

We aren't told how the world's most famous wrestling
match began, but the stands were empty when someone
confronted Jacob in a personal, private attack that lasted
until dawn! Jacob realized he was wrestling Someone
greater than himself, for he refused to let go until his Opponent blessed him. Hosea 12:4 says he "wept and
pleaded." Jacob was never the same again, physically or
spiritually. The fight was a turning point in his life and a
turning point in world history. His name was changed to
Israel. He was less selfish and deceptive, and he walked
away with a limp because of the hip injury he suffered.
Jacob encountered God in a body and he named the place
Peniel ("face of God"). God in a body is Jesus!

Why did Jesus attack Jacob? In spite of all his problems, Jacob still hadn't come to the end of his deceitful,
conniving self. He had to learn to depend entirely upon
God and not upon his own craftiness. If he failed to depend upon God, Esau would destroy him and God's plan
to bless mankind through him would be thwarted. He had
to know his own weakness and God's power. His pride
had to be destroyed and his tenacity in prayer tested.

101

Kinder says that God "would have all of Jacob's will to win, to attain and obtain, yet purged of self-sufficiency and redirected to the proper object of man's love, God Himself."

Who won? Both! Jacob resisted, then clung to Jesus. He persisted in prayer for God's blessing. God would fight for Israel! These words greatly encouraged the Israelites as they entered Canaan years later! They knew they would overcome by faith alone. The Lord wrenched Jacob's hip, a reminder that He had allowed Jacob to prevail. He asked Jacob his name, forcing Jacob ("deceiver") to admit his true nature before changing it to Israel ("God fights").

Jacob lost his self-confidence and he saw the futility of his carnal weapons. He became more bold in faith. It took all night, but he finally submitted to Someone he could not defeat. His endurance was rewarded. He became publicly effective with men only when he encountered God privately.

Maybe you have relied upon yourself for too long. You cannot live life in your own strength. All you can do in your hurt and frustration is cling to God as Jacob did. God loves it when we hold on to Him until He blesses us. Persistence in prayer pays off (Luke 18:7). Maybe God is challenging you! The Father loves a good bout in prayer with His children!

Two Changed Hearts

But Esau ran to meet Jacob and embraced him; he threw his arms around his neck and kissed him. And they wept.
Genesis 33:4

IN 2002, A REPORTER asked Arizona Diamondbacks pitcher Curt Schilling if he was angry with Barry Bonds. Schilling admitted, "We had a falling out," but added, "When I became a Christian back in 1997, I lost the ability to hate anybody." Clearly, Curt had a changed heart!

The sun rose over the horizon as Jacob limped away from Peniel. Suddenly, Esau appeared with his 400 men! Jacob quickly arranged his wives and children to meet the advancing army. He placed his favorite wife and child (Rachel and Joseph) in the rear. Maybe they would survive a slaughter. Then he went ahead, bowing seven times as he approached his estranged brother. But God had changed Esau's heart! He ran to meet his twin. They embraced and wept. Jacob was greatly relieved when he saw Esau's attitude! God suddenly and surprisingly changed him! Jacob insisted that Esau keep the droves of animals he sent to pacify his wrath. The Lord had drastically changed Jacob, too! Wealthy Esau accepted the gifts because it would be insulting to reject them.

Esau wanted to lead Jacob to his home in Seir ("wooded area"). But Jacob, knowing their approaches to life had been so different, desired to live apart from his brother. A future conflict could easily disturb their harmony. He even refused protection from Esau's troops. Accordingly, he lied to Esau by saying he would come to Seir. But he had no such intention. As soon as Esau left, Jacob went west to Succoth. Later, he settled in Shechem, where he bought land and built an altar. He named it "Mighty is the God of Israel."

Jacob was just learning to live by faith. Twenty years earlier, he had vowed to establish God's house in Bethel. A few years later, God would have to remind him of his vow. Meanwhile, tragedy struck in Shechem.

Dinah's Walk on the Wild Side

When Shechem son of Hamor the Hivite, the ruler of that area, saw her, he took her and violated her.

Genesis 34:2

STEVE DALKOWSKI HAD GREAT POTENTIAL as a Baltimore Orioles minor league pitcher. He may have been one of the fastest pitchers who ever lived. One year, he struck out 262 batters in only 170 innings for Stockton in the California league. But wildness was his problem. The same year, he walked 262 batters! One sportswriter said he could throw a ball through a barn door — except he couldn't hit the door! As fast as he was, Steve Dalkowski never pitched an inning of Major League baseball. His wildness cost him a great career.

Instead of immediately going to Bethel (30 miles away) to fulfill his vow to God, Jacob settled for ten years near a city called Shechem. His dysfunctional family lived a soap opera, with no mention of God. The wildness of his teenage daughter Dinah, who was 15 or 16, cost Jacob and his family dearly. Evidently, Dinah was socially alone. According to Josephus, she attended a pagan festival of the Canaanites. Maybe her excursion resembled the barhopping of some people today! She was in the wrong place and an ungodly man named Shechem, son of the area ruler (Hamor), raped her. Then he spoke secretly to her about marriage. His father went to Jacob with money for a dowry and a request for widespread intermarriage of their clans. It was Satan's first attempt to dilute and destroy the young nation of Israel. Evidently, rape was no big deal to the ungodly Canaanites. But Dinah's brothers were furious. To them, Hamor was merely paying for a prostitute (v. 31). Jacob seemed passive about the whole issue. He was failing miserably as a father. Jacob first neglected, then abdicated his role as leader of his family.

A problem avoided isn't a problem solved, and Jacob's sons plotted a scheme of deception, vengeance, blasphemy and murder. In proposing that Hamor's clan became circumcised before they intermarried, they used a religious ceremony to set up a slaughter. Hamor called a "town meeting" to convince his people to comply. His intent was to take all of Jacob's possessions. Like Mark Twain, who professed Christianity to marry a Christian girl, the Shechemites put on a false front.

Three days after their surgeries, the Shechemites were in pain with fever and inflammation. Dinah's full brothers (Levi and Simeon) entered their city, went house to house, killed every man, and took Dinah home in a two-man war. McGee says their slaughter made a gang shooting in Chicago look tame! Then Dinah's half-brothers looted Shechem.

Jacob knew more trouble was around the corner, for if the other Canaanite tribes united, they could exterminate Israel. He failed to instruct his family in God's ways and he maintained poor discipline at home. Four wives and mothers complicated his life. Though he later awarded no land in Canaan to Simeon and Levi (45:5-7), it was too late. All of Leah's children were involved in sin. Instead of being an example of truth and love, he was associated with deception and treachery. Like father, like sons! He was self-centered and stumbling in his walk with God. In fact, God was not even mentioned in this sordid chapter of Jacob's life. He used seven personal pronouns in verse 30 alone! His spiritual growth was a long, slow process.

BACK TO BETHEL

Then God said to Jacob, "Go up to Bethel and settle there, and build an altar to God, who appeared to you when you were fleeing from your brother Esau."

Genesis 35:1

HARRY CHITI WAS INVOLVED in the most unusual return to his former team. He was acquired by the Mets from Cleveland in 1962 for cash and a player to be named at the end of the season. The season dragged on for the inept Mets. Chiti struggled as badly as the team. At season's end, Chiti was returned to Cleveland to complete the trade. Harry Chiti had been traded for himself!

Jacob had to return to Bethel, for God takes every vow seriously (Ecclesiastes 5:4). Thirty-seven years ago, he had made a vow to God when he was running away from Esau. From his nighttime stop at Bethel (12 miles north of Jerusalem), Jacob began a personal relationship with God, who gave him several promises. Jacob had even erected a stone of remembrance at Bethel. But in the 10 years since he returned to Canaan, Jacob avoided returning to Bethel, settling 30 miles away near Shechem. At Shechem, his family was polluted by the world and his daughter was raped. Now, God reminded Jacob of his vow! He must return to Bethel.

Jacob obeyed God and moved to Bethel, where he should have lived in the first place. He buried all the pagan gods which had crept into his family, beginning with Rachel's theft of Laban's idols. He rid his family of earrings (pagan symbols of idolatry in that day) and confirmed his allegiance to God.

Almighty God repeated His promises to Israel (Jacob). He gave a large area of the Middle East to Israel and has said so many times. Whenever Jacob (Israel) kept the worship of Jehovah God his highest priority, things went well

107

for him and his family. After 10 rough years in Shechem, his priorities were being restored.

God struck so much fear in the hearts of Israel's enemies, that Jacob had no need to fear retaliation for the deeds of his two wild sons. Before he put away sin in his house, Jacob feared his neighbors. Now, they feared him! The Lord appeared to Jacob again at Bethel, where Jacob constructed an altar for sacrifice.

Do you need to go "back to Bethel"? Maybe you've wandered far from your previously close relationship with the living God. He is calling you back right now. If you'll obey Him and return, He'll restore the joy of living!

THE SOCIAL SECTION

Isaac lived a hundred and eighty years. Then he breathed his last and died and was gathered to his people, old and full of years. And his sons Esau and Jacob buried him.

Genesis 35:28-29

THE LATTER PART OF GENESIS 35 resembles the social section of a modern newspaper. Recorded here are several deaths in Jacob's family, the birth of Benjamin, and the scandal of Reuben.

News item #1: Jacob moved from Bethel to Hebron (Mamre), which was 22 miles south of Jerusalem. No reason is given. He was approximately 105 years old.

News item #2: On the way to Hebron (near Bethlehem), Rachel gave birth to a son. During the terribly difficult delivery, she died. As Rachel breathed her last, she named her son Ben-oni ("son of my trouble"). But Jacob renamed him Benjamin ("son of the right hand"). Benjamin pictures both the suffering of the Lord Jesus Christ and His eventual glory as He sits at the right hand of the Father in heaven. Rachel's grave stone was still in place 400 years later, when Israel came from Egypt! It remains in place today!

News item #3: Rebekah's nurse Deborah died (v. 8). She was approximately 180 years old and had probably cared for Jacob when he was a child. Deborah was greatly honored, and she had probably come to live with Jacob once Rebekah died. There was great sorrow upon her death, for her burial site under an oak tree was named Allon Bacuth ("oak of weeping").

News item #4: Scandal! Jacob's son, Reuben, slept with Jacob's concubine-wife, Bilhah. Because of this evil deed, Reuben lost the blessing of his birthright as oldest son (49:3-4) and it was given to Joseph (I Chronicles 5:1-

109

2). The problems associated with polygamy never seem to go away. Jacob was partial to Rachel and her sons and evidently received little joy from his other 10 boys.

News item #5: Isaac died at the age of 180. He had been blind and feeble since age 137. The fact that he was "gathered to his people" indicates the eternal nature of his soul and his reuniting with those who knew and loved God!

News item #6: The twins, Jacob and Esau, were once again together at their father's funeral. Our heavenly Father, who does all things well, peacefully reunited the two radically different brothers.

DIFFERENT DESTINATIONS

Esau took his wives and sons and daughters and all the members of his household, as well as his livestock and all his other animals and all the goods he had acquired in Canaan, and moved to a land some distance from his brother Jacob.

Genesis 36:6

MAX FLACK AND CLIFTON HEATHCOTE were two Major League ballplayers headed in different directions. On May 30, 1922, the Chicago Cubs traded Flack to the St Louis Cardinals for Heathcote. The two players became the only men in Major League history to compete for two different teams in one day!

Jacob and Esau, though twins, were as different as night and day. Their destinations in life were in opposite directions. While Jacob was interested in serving God, Esau was a man of the flesh. He was an outdoorsman, but he had no desire for truth, character, or other eternal values. He married three pagan wives, who surely didn't draw him closer to God. He became father of the Edomites, Arabs whose ranks swelled to 100,000 strong enemies of Israel. The long line of their pagan chiefs is listed in Genesis 36. Material prosperity, which came quickly, was theirs. But they had no interest in spiritual greatness, which takes more time, patience, and obedience.

Esau moved further away from Jacob to find enough pasture land for his expanding herds. He evidently conquered the area near Mt. Seir, a 500-foot peak south of the Dead Sea (Deuteronomy 2:5; Joshua 24:4). Cut out of rock, the city of Petra became their capitol as they spread all the way into North Africa. They established chiefs and kings to rule themselves under the "overlord" Esau. Not one of Esau's descendants is listed as faithful to God. They had worldly wealth and power, but no interest in God.

111

Their independent spirit told them they didn't need God. Obediah 1:3-4 reveals their prideful nature. Over 1,000 years after Esau lived, God revealed that He knew Esau's heart all along (Malachi 1:1-5).

God details the ancestry of the Arabs in His Word. Though they aren't chosen to reveal God to the world and they are aliens in the land of Israel, like anyone else they can individually be saved by receiving the Lord Jesus Christ.

What a gracious God we serve!

JOSEPH'S LONG TRIP

Judah said to his brothers, "What will we gain if we kill our brother and cover up his blood? Come, let's sell him to the Ishmaelites and not lay our hands on him; after all, he is our brother, our own flesh and blood." His brothers agreed.
Genesis 37:26-27

ROAD TRIPS REQUIRE TEAMS to make adjustments in routine. Time zones change, meal schedules can be disrupted, and sleeping becomes erratic. Most teams would much rather play at home before a friendly crowd. It seems the longer the road trip, the more days it takes for players to make the adjustment necessary to play well.

Joseph's brothers sent him on a long road trip against his will. This one trip determined the course of his life. He was 17 years old, possibly somewhat spoiled and arrogant, and hated by his brothers. They grew extremely jealous of their father's favoritism of Joseph. The brothers were morally impure and Joseph's innocence was a source of irritation. Furthermore, when Joseph unwisely shared his dreams with them, they added envy to their hatred!

The 10 older brothers had taken their flocks 60 miles back to Shechem to graze on land still owned by Jacob. It's possible they went on their own, without asking their father's permission. Evidently, a long period of time elapsed with no word of their fate. Shechem was a dangerous place for them after their earlier slaughter of people in the area. Eventually, Jacob decided to send Joseph to see how they were doing.

Unaware of the deep hatred of his brothers, Joseph obediently started on his way to Shechem — a journey of about two days. When he arrived there, the brothers were nowhere to be found. A stranger told him they had gone another 20 miles to Dothan ("two cisterns"), where there were two storage wells. They were far from home, searching for greener pastures, and confronted by at least one dry well. Joseph had no idea of the trauma awaiting him as he approached Dothan and his half-brothers.

As Joseph came into view, his bright coat, flashed like a red flag waved in front of an angry bull! The brothers recognized him and hurriedly discussed a plan to kill him. Older brother Reuben, who would have to answer to Jacob, dissented. He convinced the others to throw Joseph into the dry well. In great distress, Joseph earnestly pleaded for his life (Genesis 42:21). The fall into the well was probably a violent one, but there were evidently no bones broken.

As the brothers sat down to eat, Reuben left the scene. In the providence of God, a caravan of Ishmaelites/ Midianites appeared in the distance. These people were distant relatives of Jacob who were headed to Egypt on a trade mission. Judah expressed the bright idea of selling Joseph to them for profit. They could be rid of Joseph and make money at the same time! So, they sold him for 20 silver coins.

Reuben was alarmed when he returned and discovered Joseph gone. He confronted his brothers and they all agreed to deceive their father by dipping Joseph's coat in animal blood to imply that he was dead. How deeply deception ran in Jacob's family! Jacob believed the lie and refused to be comforted. He was not yet walking by faith and now he had lost the son most fit for spiritual leadership of the family and the future nation.

The Ishmaelites/Midianites sold 17-year-old Joseph to a prominent Egyptian official named Potiphar ("one whom Ra, the sun god, has given"), who was possibly the chief executioner for Pharaoh. The Hebrew word translated "officer" is "saris," meaning "eunuch," which may explain much that later transpired around his house!

God had told Abraham He would send Israel into slavery until the pagans in Canaan had an extended opportunity to repent of their sin (Genesis 15:13-16). The events in Joseph's life set His plan in motion, but Joseph had no way of knowing about the great things ahead of him. From what he could see, his visions were dead. In his own power, he would never realize their fulfillment. He had to trust in a sovereign God who has ultimate good in mind for His people. This long road trip tested Joseph to the limit!

There are many lessons to be learned from Genesis 37. Jacob's partiality put Joseph in a difficult position. Joseph's telling everything he had heard from God to people with no "spiritual ears" increased their hatred of him. Jacob's deception of his own father was repeated by his children back to him. The brothers' hatred of a person of character in their family has been repeated many times in history. Finally, the providence of a sovereign God who causes or allows all things to happen both amazes and confounds us. As Matthew Henry says, "God's provinces often seem to contradict His purposes, even when they are serving them."

What a wise, omnipotent God we serve!

ONE TANGLED MESS

*Judah recognized them and said, "She is more righteous
than I, since I wouldn't give her to my son Shelah."*
Genesis 38:26

TWO BOSTON RED SOX STARS, each concerned with their
own statistics, once created a tangled mess. Five-time
American League batting champion Wade Boggs persuaded
a scorekeeper to change an error he had charged to Boggs
on defense. That upset ace pitcher Roger Clemens, who
was, therefore, charged with an earned run!

During the 22 years that Joseph was in Egypt before
his family arrived (Genesis 47), Israel became a tangled
mess. Chapter 38 reveals the sordid affairs of Judah. It
demonstrates the need to get God's chosen line away from
the degrading influence of the Canaanites.

Judah married a Canaanite wife and fathered three
sons. One of them (Er) married a woman named Tamar.
Er became so wicked that God killed him. Custom dictated that a dead man's brother sire children with the
brother's wife so his family line could continue. But Onan,
Er's brother, selfishly refused to father children with Tamar.
So God also killed him and Tamar went back to her pagan
family to wait for Judah's third son to mature so he could
continue her family line.

When Tamar realized Judah had no intention of allow-
ing her family line to continue, she set a trap for him.
Ritual sex with shrine prostitutes in Canaan was performed
at sheep shearing time. It supposedly brought good fortune. Tamar posed as a prostitute and entrapped Judah,
whose own wife had died. When she was discovered to be
pregnant, Judah, as head of the family, pronounced judgment. As Tamar was about to be burned to death, she
revealed to everyone that Judah was the father of her child!
An embarrassed Judah repealed his harsh edict. He could
see the sin of Tamar, but was blind to his own sin.

The Canaanites are gone today. God judged and removed them from the earth. But Matthew 1:3 reveals that Tamar and one of her twin sons, Perez, are in the legal genealogy of Jesus Christ through Joseph, his legal guardian! How amazing that God would take the tangled mess of Israel's family and use it for good!

SUCCESS IN HUMILIATION

The warden paid no attention to anything under Joseph's care, because the LORD was with Joseph and gave him success in whatever he did.

Genesis 39:23

IN 1976, DOUG DECINCES replaced a legend, Brooks Robinson, at third base for the Baltimore Orioles. No matter how well he played over the next six years, all that mattered to fans was that he wasn't Robinson, "the Vacuum Cleaner." Even when he hit 28 home runs in 1978, he got mostly one kind of mail: hate mail.

"The experience made me a stronger player and probably helped me stay in the game as long as I did," he said. "I grew from it."

Like Doug DeCinces, Joseph was rejected by his own people and he grew from it. Enslaved by Gentiles, Joseph's character shined like a bright light in a dark world. In all the adversity of slavery and prison, God was with him and granted him success. Joseph's trials were merely stepping stones to becoming prime minister of Egypt. His humiliation resulted in his exaltation! In this sense, his life resembled the life of the Lord Jesus Christ!

As a 17-year-old slave, Joseph was sold to Potiphar, an officer (saris" = "eunuch") of Pharaoh who may have been chief executioner. Day after day, Joseph resisted the advances of Potiphar's promiscuous wife. He called her proposals by the proper name: sin. He pointed out that sin is against God. He ran from it (II Timothy 2:22). He could have rationalized, for adultery was condoned in pagan culture. When she falsely accused him of attempted rape, Joseph didn't defend himself. His character was being refined through trial (I Peter 2:19-23). Though angry, Potiphar may have suspected his wife and didn't kill Joseph because of her sexual looseness. It's possible the other servants didn't believe her either.

Even in prison with neck irons and foot shackles (Psalm 105:18-19), God was with Joseph (vv. 3, 21), gave him success and favor (vv. 3, 4, 21, 23), blessed him (v. 5), and showed him kindness (v. 21). God never appeared to Joseph as He did to the other patriarchs, but Joseph knew He was near!

Joseph suffered through the death of his dreams. There was no way he could fulfill the dreams himself. God would have to do it, if they were to be fulfilled. But God's way up is often down. Joseph's path to the throne went through prison as a loving God worked all things together for good (Romans 8:28). He does the same in our lives. All our heartaches and sufferings are used by God for His glory and our ultimate good! Someone has said, "God nothing does, nor suffers (allows) to be done, but what we would do ourselves, if we but could see through all events of life as well as He."

Futility of Self-Help

The chief cupbearer, however, did not remember Joseph; he forgot him.

Genesis 40:23

THE CHICAGO CUBS have developed a reputation as lovable losers. Their game on May 17, 1979, illustrates the frustration often felt by the team and their fans. Philadelphia led the Cubs by seven runs before they even came to bat, and by 21-9 after 4$_{F(1,2)}$ innings. But the Cubs swung away and finally tied the score 22-22 in the 8th inning, only to lose the game on Mike Schmidt's 10th-inning home run! The Cubs seemed unable to help themselves to victory in spite of 22 runs.

Joseph was a slave/prisoner for 13 years. He was 17 when sold into Egypt and 30 when made prime minister. It seemed like a long time for a proud, intelligent young man to "waste" in captivity, but it was God's training program for him. Joseph failed in his effort to help himself escape. He would be released only in God's time.

Joseph glorified God and served others during his own adversity (v. 8). He may have occasionally become discouraged, but he remained faithful to God. He became humble and sensitive to the feelings of others (vv. 6-7). Pharaoh's chief cupbearer and chief baker had been accused of crimes against Pharaoh, possibly of attempted poisoning or negligence in protecting him. They were imprisoned until their cases could be investigated. When they had disturbing dreams, God gave Joseph the interpretations. The cupbearer, like Joseph, was innocent. Joseph asked for his help to be released, but the cupbearer forgot him.

Humanly speaking, there was no hope for Joseph. The cupbearer who oversaw the king's vineyards (and probably hundreds of workers) had forgotten him. But God hadn't forgotten. He was right where God wanted him. It's a good thing he wasn't released, for he probably would have returned to Canaan. Two years later, when Pharaoh had his dream, the cupbearer's memory "returned" and Joseph was summoned. Events moved rapidly as Pharaoh elevated Joseph to the second-highest office in Egypt!

Are you discouraged in your humble circumstances? Promotion comes from God (Psalm 75:6-7). He does a much better job than we can do. Self-help is often counterproductive. Be content with your calling in life and God will exalt you in His way and time!

God Promotes Joseph

Then Pharaoh took his signet ring from his finger and put it on Joseph's finger. He dressed him in robes of fine linen and put a gold chain around his neck. He had him ride in a chariot as his second in command, and men shouted before him, "Make way!" Thus he put him in charge of the whole land of Egypt.

Genesis 41:42-43

THE ST. LOUIS RAMS began 1999 with the worst record of the '90s. Their quarterback, Kurt Warner, had worked the night shift stocking shelves at a supermarket only five years earlier. Yet, he led the team to victory in the Super Bowl!

"I believe the Lord has a plan for each of us that's better than anything we can imagine — even if that plan isn't obvious to us at every stage," Warner said. "He prepared me for this over a long period of time — in lower-profile locker rooms and the grocery store and in Europe, through all the personal tragedies and in spite of the people who doubted me all the way!"

Two years after Joseph helped the cupbearer in prison, God was ready to promote Joseph. He sent two dreams to Pharaoh. None of Egypt's Satanic magicians could interpret them, for they came from God! Finally, the cupbearer remembered Joseph and his ability to interpret dreams. Joseph was quickly summoned and cleaned up (Egyptians were noted for cleanliness and clean shaves).

Joseph gave glory to God as the revealer of dreams. He didn't try to bargain with Pharaoh. He had grown much since his own boyhood dreams and now he was humble and patient. He was neither bitter nor vindictive after years of slavery and prison. God revealed that seven years of plenty would be followed by seven years of worldwide famine. He even gave Joseph a strategy for survival.

Egypt was accustomed to prosperity and the dreams alarmed Pharaoh ("The Ra"). Pharaohs considered themselves agents of Ra (the sun god), the god of Egypt. This particular Pharaoh was probably one of the Hyksos ("shepherd rulers"), nomadic Bedouins who conquered and governed Egypt for a time. They had understandable difficulty with the loyalty of Egyptians, and Joseph may have been closer in ancestry to this Pharaoh than any Egyptian. In any case, God turned the heart of Pharaoh to Joseph (Proverbs 21:1). He made Joseph second in command of all Egypt, the world's most powerful nation.

Joseph was given a new name and an Egyptian wife. He had two sons during the seven years of plenty. Their names, Manasseh ("forget") and Ephriam ("twice fruitful"), indicate that God made Joseph forget his troubled past and that He had prospered Joseph. Joseph never forsook a Godly worldview in spite of temptation, suffering, and paganism all around him. Prison had become a fast track to power. God had destroyed his dreams to fulfill them! Joseph hadn't lobbied or manipulated his way to the throne, yet God had prepared him without his awareness of it. He was a man of integrity whose head could not be turned by pride or prosperity. His troubles turned out for his own good and for the salvation of the world!

GOD BREAKS THE CYCLE OF DECEIT

Now Joseph was the governor of the land, the one who sold grain to all its people. So when Joseph's brothers arrived, they bowed down to him with their faces to the ground.
Genesis 42:6

ON AUGUST 3, 1987, UMPIRES suspected that Minnesota Twins pitcher Joe Niekro was doctoring baseballs. However, they had difficulty catching him. Finally, they ordered Joe to empty his pockets. When he turned a back pocket inside out, a five-inch emery board flew out! Niekro was ejected from the game and suspended for 10 games. His deceit was uncovered and dealt with.

Wealthy Jacob (Israel) had to do something. All his money couldn't buy grain that didn't exist in Canaan! The family was starving in the famine. Even though living in the Promised Land, Jacob — like Abraham and Isaac — experienced famines to test his faith and to keep his eyes upon Heaven (Hebrews 11:13-16). Now God began to break the cycle of deceit.

Jacob sent 10 of his sons the 250 miles to Egypt so they could buy grain. He kept Benjamin home, fearful of losing his remaining favorite son. When the brothers arrived in Egypt, they bowed down to none other than Joseph! Prophecy was fulfilled and Joseph recognized it as he recalled his boyhood dreams (v. 9). Joseph was now over 37 years old. He spoke, looked, and acted like an Egyptian. His brothers weren't looking for him and didn't recognize him! They were speaking to a person they thought was dead!

God worked to break Jacob's cycle of deception! He used Joseph, who first sought to determine his brothers' attitudes toward God and family. Accordingly, he harshly accused them of spying. Indeed, all alien travelers had to be screened, for Egypt had the only grain in the whole region. Through an interpreter, he "whip-sawed" the brothers back and forth, throwing them into prison for three days, then sending all except Simeon (who had been a cruel man) home to bring Benjamin back. Joseph wanted to know the truth about Benjamin. He returned their silver in their grain sacks. Joseph never missed giving glory to God (v. 18). Knowing the famine would last several more years, he knew they would return.

Joseph's means of awakening his brothers' seared moral consciousness was working. For all they knew, they could spend the rest of their lives in an Egyptian prison. Their sensitivity to God was returning. "What is this that God has done to us?" they asked (v. 28). The process of repentance had begun. Their fear became even greater when they returned home (v. 35)!

God was at work in Jacob's life, too. At the age of 130, he was still very weak in faith. "Everything is against me!" he exclaimed (v. 36). Though he was no longer a cocky youth, he was still not a man of great faith, nor were most of his sons. But God was changing him. Ultimately, everything would work together for His glory and Jacob's good!

"The Man"

Take your brother also and go back to the man at once. And may God Almighty grant you mercy before the man so that he will let your other brother and Benjamin come back with you. As for me, if I am bereaved, I am bereaved.

Genesis 43:13-14

STAN MUSIAL was one of the greatest hitters of all time. During his stellar Major League career with the St. Louis Cardinals, Musial earned the nickname "The Man." In a 1954 doubleheader, Stan "The Man" Musial became the first Major Leaguer to hit five home runs in one day! He did it at Old Sportsman's Park in St. Louis.

Joseph was "The Man" in Egypt, sent there by God to save Israel during the seven-year famine. Jacob didn't recognize God's sovereign work behind the scenes, but the Lord used the threat of starvation to get the family out of the paganism of Canaan for the next 400 years! Jacob (Israel) had to learn to trust God before the nation could reveal Him to the world! "The Man" was the key to their salvation.

Facing starvation, faithless Jacob was squeezed into a corner (v. 14). MacArthur says, "Pessimism had apparently set into his heart and deepened after the loss of Joseph." Simeon remained a prisoner in Egypt. "The Man" wanted to see Benjamin. Judah finally convinced Jacob to let Benjamin return to Egypt with the brothers to obtain more grain. Maybe his conscience was starting to bother him (42:21). For 20 years, the brothers had lived with the deep, dark secret of what they had done to Joseph.

The 10 brothers had sold Joseph for 20 pieces of silver. Now they took 20 *bundles* of money to buy grain from him! When they arrived in Egypt, God turned up the heat another degree, for Joseph invited (required) them to eat at his house. They feared he would rob and enslave them.

Evidently, Joseph had told his steward about God (v. 23), for it was to him the brothers apologized, explained, and plead the case of the returned money. Twice more, the 10 brothers bowed low to Joseph, fulfilling his God-given childhood dreams. When Joseph seated them by birth order, things really became eerie. The odds were 40 million to one against their being randomly seated in this way, but they still didn't recognize Joseph! God was dealing with their hearts, demonstrating that He was in ultimate control.

Joseph had Benjamin served five times as much as the others. If the brothers had any resentment toward Benjamin (as they had had toward Joseph), it surely would surface. They were being tested in ways they didn't understand!

"The Man" wept often during the process of revealing himself. He had a heart of love toward those who had hated and rejected him. More than any other man, Joseph pictures the Lord Jesus Christ, who loved us before we even knew Him! "The Man" had been the object of scorn, but no one was laughing now!

A FINAL CHARACTER TEST

Now then, please let your servant remain here as my lord's slave in place of the boy, and let the boy return with his brothers. How can I go back to my father if the boy isn't with me? No! Do not let me see the misery that would come upon my father.

Genesis 44:33-34

JOE MONTANA EXHIBITED the character qualities necessary to lead great football teams. He not only shared credit; but he also accepted blame. When he received a bad snap from center, he'd tell the coach it was his own fault, even if it meant getting chewed out.

"When you're a leader, you've got to be willing to take the blame," he said. "People appreciate when you're not pointing fingers at them, because that just adds to their pressure. If you can get past that, you can talk about fixing what went wrong."

God repeatedly conducts tests of character, just as He did in the days of Jacob and his family. He used Joseph in a final test of the attitude of Jacob's 10 sons. When they left Egypt for Canaan with full sacks of corn, Joseph ordered his personal cup placed into Benjamin's sack and their money refunded. Then he had them arrested!

Joseph's insight came from God, but he probably used the cup as a prop to further convince the brothers that he was Egyptian. The brothers were extremely distraught. They knew God had uncovered their guilt of selling Joseph 22 years earlier (v. 16) and they confessed their sins. Their attitudes were changed! They could have used the occasion to get rid of young Benjamin ("favored one") as they had done to Joseph. Years earlier, they didn't care how their father felt. But now, they loved and respected Jacob (v. 20), who still didn't have the faith to continue living if he lost Benjamin! They would stand with Benjamin, dying with him if necessary.

Back in Egypt, they bowed before Joseph for the fourth time. Judah interceded for his youngest brother in one of the most moving petitions of Scripture. Judah was not the same man seen in chapters 37-38. As spokesman from now on, he offered himself in exchange for the life of his brother and for the sake of his father. What a picture of the Lord Jesus Christ (Hebrews 7:14), the "Lion of the Tribe of Judah." Benjamin's descendants were forever grateful to Judah, supporting his tribe when everyone else forsook it.

The brothers passed Joseph's tests and grew through them. They were now of one mind. They were sorry for their sin. Before, they hadn't cared for Joseph's cries or Jacob's grief. Now, they were changed. They would remain a part of the fulfillment of God's promises!

What if the brothers had failed? What if they had been unrepentant and forsaken Benjamin? God could have destroyed them all and still fulfilled His promises through Joseph. Their growth in grace was for their own good!

How has God tested you? Have you passed or failed His character tests? The consequences are enormous! If you trust Him, you'll enjoy His blessing. If not, there is still time to change your attitude (repent) and submit to Him.

GOD'S PURPOSE IS FINALLY REVEALED

But God sent me ahead of you to preserve for you a remnant on earth and to save your lives by a great deliverance.

Genesis 45:7

JOE TORRE WAITED 4,272 GAMES as a player and manager to get to the World Series, His was the longest wait in history. Finally, he managed the Yankees in the 1996 Series and he has since been in many more. "It has been tough watching the Series," said Torre before his first Series game. "Mostly I turned it off. It's like watching someone else eat a hot-fudge sundae. And that's not fun."

Joseph's wait was finally over. He could now reveal both his identity and God's purpose to his brothers. Judah's passionate plea, his confession, and his self-sacrifice convinced Joseph that the brothers' repentance was genuine. He cleared the room, possibly to the consternation of his Egyptian bodyguards. The vile deeds of the brothers were not for the ears of others. No longer using an interpreter, Joseph boldly declared in Hebrew, "I am Joseph!" His brothers thought his name was Zaphenath-Paneah. He wept loudly. Joseph had been away from his brothers for 22 years. He was 39 years old.

The brothers were terrified! They feared he would kill them. But Joseph revealed a God-centered worldview. Three times (vv. 5-9) he said, "God sent me ahead to save lives." He knew God is Sovereign (Psalm 105:17). He knew God had promised to make a great nation of Jacob's descendants. He could forgive because God was calling all the shots. He hadn't asked for his powerful position. Israel didn't seek favor with Pharaoh and the Egyptians (vv. 16-20). God gave it. On a human level, Pharaoh was probably overjoyed to have more loyal subjects like Joseph. But God was at work to save Israel. He removed them from the evil influence of the Canaanites for the next 400 years!

Pharaoh instructed Israel to sell everything and move to Goshen, a 40-mile-long valley in the Northeast Nile Delta near Memphis. The area was great for livestock and isolated from most Egyptians. There, Israel multiplied and retained her identity.

"Don't quarrel (v. 24)!" warned Joseph, as his brothers left to get Jacob. They would have much to contemplate as they discussed how to confess their sin to their father. The "blame game" would not help anyone! Their main message to Jacob was, "He's alive and we're forgiven!" Stunned, the 130-year-old Jacob was revived in spirit (v. 27). He lived 17 more years in Egypt!

Like Joseph, the resurrected Lord Jesus Christ will one day reveal Himself to his "brothers" (Israel) who have rejected Him! "They will look on me, the one they have pierced, and they will mourn for him as one mourns for an only child, and grieve bitterly for him as one grieves for a firstborn son" (Zechariah 12:10)! God works everything out for His eternal purposes. His ways are beyond our understanding. That's because He's God and we're not!

A FRESH VISION

"I am God, the God of your father," he said. "Do not be afraid to go down to Egypt, for I will make you into a great nation there. I will go down to Egypt with you, and I will surely bring you back again. And Joseph's own hand will close your eyes."

Genesis 46:3-4

THE 1908 GEORGIA BULLDOGS were fearful and intimidated. During a scoreless game with Tennessee, they had moved the football to the Vols' two-yard line when a grizzled mountaineer, reeking of sour mash, strode into their huddle and fingered a .38 revolver!

"The first man who crosses the goal line will get a bullet in his carcass," he declared, before police hustled him away.

The Bulldogs fumbled on the next play and never threatened again, losing 10-0.

Joseph's invitation to come to Egypt wasn't sufficient to overcome Jacob's fear. He needed a word from God and he received one. At the age of 130 years, Jacob packed everything in a wagon train and set out for Egypt. This time, he wasn't running away from someone or walking in his own strength. Arriving at Beersheba, a favorite dwelling place of both Abraham and Isaac, Jacob offered sacrifices in worship of God. The Lord had told Isaac *not* to go to Egypt, and Abraham had had a terrible experience there. Two hundred fifteen years earlier, God had promised to make Abraham into a great nation. Yet, there were only 70 people in Jacob's "nation" now. Jacob needed the encouragement of a fresh vision.

A fresh vision is what Jacob got! For the eighth (and last) time, God spoke to him in a vision, giving Jacob a "green light" to go to Egypt.

Joseph met his father in Goshen and it was an emotional reunion. Joseph seemed "back from the dead" to old Jacob. They had been separated for 22 years! The old man could die in peace.

Unashamed to be called their brother, Joseph coached his brothers in speaking to Pharaoh. They were shepherds; and the Egyptians hated shepherds! Being more culturally and intellectually advanced at the time, the Egyptians considered themselves superior. It was a clear case of discrimination! Israel was given the land of Goshen, where they would be isolated from the Egyptians. They raised livestock and retained their identity as a small nation. Over the years, they became a great nation! They learned much from the Egyptians in their 430 years outside the land of Canaan.

SUCCESS AWAY FROM HOME

Now the Israelites settled in Egypt in the region of Goshen. They acquired property there and were fruitful and increased greatly in number.

Genesis 47:27

MOST TEAMS FARE MUCH BETTER at home than on the road. The home field is an advantage because it's familiar, the crowd is partial, and travel hasn't sapped their energy. If a team has a winning record away from home, it's a real bonus. Such teams will probably enjoy an outstanding season!

Israel's "team" enjoyed great success on the road in Egypt, even during a famine. The nation prospered because God had told them to go to Egypt and they obeyed Him. Pharaoh treated them kindly, and he also was blessed. Throughout Scripture blessings are upon those who treat Israel well and curses are upon those who treat the nation poorly!

Old Jacob blessed Pharaoh. From God's viewpoint, Jacob was greater than Pharaoh, for the greater always blesses the lesser (Hebrews 7:7). Jacob was 130 years old when he entered Egypt and he had 17 more years to live. His life had been short (in comparison to his father's) and difficult. Most of his calamity, distress, and anguish he brought upon himself. He acted as his own worst enemy! He hadn't a thing of which to boast. But he had become a changed man and his best days were ahead! Jacob was finally living by faith (v. 31)! As he believed God's promises by faith, he worshipped God. Hebrews 11:21 selects this act of worship as Jacob's great act of faith. He is the only hero of faith commended as a worshiper in the "faith" chapter! Years earlier, Jacob had tried to gain God's blessing by deception. What a change had taken place!

Joseph was a loyal administrator for Pharaoh. The Egyptian people wanted to trade their land and their labor to his government for food when they ran out of money and livestock. They trusted Joseph. Instead of giving them free food (socialism), he allowed them to keep their self-respect. He saved their lives and they were grateful to their benevolent leader (v. 25). Dependence upon free government handouts would have soon bankrupted the government, destroyed the morals of the people, and resulted in anarchy. It's possible that Joseph sold the land back at the end of the famine. It's also likely that Pharaoh overruled Joseph and allowed the pagan priests to keep their land, for Egypt was a land full of superstitious religion.

With success on the road, Israel became a great nation. Her greatest days were still to come!

JACOB'S FARM SYSTEM

"They are the sons God has given me here," Joseph said to his father.
Then Israel said, "Bring them to me so I may bless them."
Genesis 48:9

A FARM SYSTEM IS DESIGNED by Major League teams for the purpose of developing players for the parent club. Those teams with solid farm systems usually succeed most often, for they have a continual source of new talent. Much time and money is spent on each succeeding crop of Major League players.

As Jacob neared death, he remembered God's promises. Joseph's sons, Ephraim and Manasseh, would become significant new players on God's "team," and Jacob passed his blessing on to these grandsons of Rachel. Jacob was finally living in his new nature. He had insights as an old man that he lacked in earlier years when living in his old fleshly nature! He had "grown" in grace and in the knowledge of God (II Peter 3:18). God had been very patient with Jacob. The old patriarch gave credit to "the angel who has redeemed ("goel") from all harm" (v. 16)! He was finally sensitive to the leading of God's Spirit!

Ephraim and Manasseh became tribes of Israel. The nation totaled 12 tribes (Levi became the priests who were scattered among the others). God blessed the younger son above the older. He paid no attention to natural birth order or customs, for God supernaturally decides who He'll bless and how He'll bless them! He blesses for spiritual reasons, not chronological ones.

Joseph's two sons received more land in Canaan than the other brothers. Both Joshua and Jeroboam came from the tribe of Ephraim, whose name became synonymous with Israel (Isaiah 7:2; Hosea 4:17, 13:1). Jacob also gave Joseph the land he had first purchased from the Amorites. They took it back by force and Jacob retook it by force! Modern Israel wants to build on this land. It's called the West Bank.

137

PRE-SEASON PREDICTIONS

*Then Jacob called for his sons and said: "gather around
so I can tell you what will happen to you in days to come."*
Genesis 49:1

SPORTSWRITERS CONDUCT POLLS of conference football coaches before each season to predict the championship team and the order of finish. Even all-conference and
all-American selections are predicted before the season
even begins. Sometimes these polls are accurate, but sometimes they aren't.

As Jacob neared death, he called his 12 sons together
and gave inspired predictions about their futures. Each
prophecy contained both a blessing and a warning. All of
them were accurate and many have now become history.

Reuben, the oldest son, was not given a position of
prominence because he had slept with Jacob's concubine,
Bilhah (Genesis 35:22). He had thrown away his virtue
and, with it, his reputation. Reuben was as unstable as
water, resembling Jacob's early life. His tribe never ex-
celled at anything. As one wag put it, "the only thing named
after Reuben was a sandwich!"

Simeon and Levi were close companions who ambushed
and killed the Shechemites out of anger for the deeds of
one of them. They were given no land, but by the grace of
God, the tribe of Levi was made a priestly tribe. Passive in
his early life, Jacob now pronounces moral judgments upon
these formerly rebellious sons.

Judah was responsible for the sale of Joseph into slavery. He had committed fornication with Tamar. But his
life was changed and his became a most remarkable tribe.
Years later, King David, Solomon, and the Lord Jesus Christ
("Shiloh") were born into the tribe of Judah! Genesis 49:8-
12 includes some of the most amazing prophecies of God's

139

Word concerning Jesus! The scepter of the universe belongs in His hands, for He created everything! When He comes again, it will be in judgment upon His enemies and His robe will be red with their blood (Isaiah 63:2-3). He will rule in a day of abundance (wine and milk). Jesus is the "Lion of the Tribe of Judah" (Revelation 5:5)!

Zebulum probably never dwelt along the Mediterranean coast, but the tribe did benefit from trade routes to the Sea. Matthew 4:13 suggests his border extended to the Sea of Galilee.

Issachar ("man of wages") was a tribe of hard workers and brave soldiers. Zebulum and Issachar became the backbone of the nation of Israel.

Dan ("judge") would be a rebellious tribe with no moral commitment. Dan became the northernmost tribe that left its original land allotment in Israel. Dan introduced idolatry into Israel on an official basis. The name "Yeshuah" (salvation) is first mentioned here by Jacob to interject hope for the salvation of God. Dan isn't mentioned in the tribal list in Revelation 7:4-8.

Gad eventually settled east of the Jordan River to protect Israel's frontier. The Gadites became tough fighters (I Chronicles 5 and 12).

Asher became successful farmers in a rich coastal region in Israel.

Naphtali became a lightning-quick military tribe. They were also eloquent of speech. Deborah and Barak came from Naphtali (Judges 4:5-6), as did all of Jesus' disciples, except Judas.

The tribes which came from Joseph — Ephraim and Manasseh — became very prominent in Israel, but they also led Israel into idol worship. Great physical blessings were promised to them. Jacob tried to call them back to God even before they fell from His favor! Their history should serve as a warning of the dangers of material prosperity.

Benjamin became warlike and cruel. This tribe developed deadly archers and stone-slingers (Judges 20; I Chronicles 8, 12; II Chronicles 14, 17). Both Saul and Paul came from Benjamin.

God has plans for Israel! A fundamental principle is that the lives and natures of the patriarchs affect their descendants. Jacob's prophesies looked forward to the settlement of the Promised Land and beyond. He had the future planned beyond the coming bondage in the land of Egypt, and He has the future of every Christian planned as well!

Jacob's Colorful Life Ends

When Jacob had finished giving instructions to his sons, he drew his feet up into the bed, breathed his last and was gathered to his people.

Genesis 49:33

BEFORE HE DIED, colorful Casy Stengel managed for 25 years in the Major Leagues. He was known as the "Old Professor" for his habit of saying, "You can look it up." Stengel managed in 10 World Series and also spent 14 years as a player. "I broke in with four hits and the writers promptly declared they had seen the new Ty Cobb," he said. "It took me only a few days to correct that impression."

Jacob had lived a very colorful life before he died at age 147. Before he died, Jacob experienced his finest years in Egypt, where he gained great honor and respect as Joseph's father. He had lived a life of self-sufficiency and deceit, but God broke down his pride at Peniel. Jacob had learned to trust God totally when he saw Joseph alive in Egypt. Though he had many faults, he had a desire to know God. Thankfully, God's faithfulness overcame Jacob's weakness.

The Egyptians publicly mourned Jacob's death for 70 days, just two days short of the official mourning period for a pharaoh! They were advanced beyond our culture in embalming techniques, and most likely used the first-class method known as "Osiris style" on Jacob. The brain was extracted through the nostrils by means of a curved iron probe and various drugs were injected into the cranium. The intestines were drawn out through a sharp incision in the side, and myrrh, cassia, and spices were substituted. The body was sewn up and placed in alkali for 70 days. Then it was wrapped with bands of fine linen, smeared with gum and laid in a wooden case in the shape of a man.

143

The case was stood upright against a wall. At one point, in the city of Thebes, one-fourth of the people were engaged in the embalming industry!

Joseph led a funeral procession to Jacob's grave site, 300 miles away in Canaan. It may have been the world's longest funeral procession and it was Joseph's first time back in that land in 39 years. Many Egyptians joined the procession and they mourned so deeply near the Jordan River that the Canaanites called the place Abel Mizraim ("Mourning of Egypt").

As the book of Genesis concludes, we can't escape the emphasis on death. Since the sin of Adam and Eve in chapter 2, death came upon all men. All of us have sinned. The wages of sin is death. We would remain in this terrible condition, except for the remedy God promised to provide. Only the fulfillment of His promise to send a Redeemer can change anything!

Read Genesis 50;15-26

HIGHER PURPOSES

You intended to harm me, but God intended it for good to accomplish what is now being done, the saving of many lives.

Genesis 50:20

AT THE HEIGHT OF HER FAME and fortune, Chris Evert was unsatisfied and searching for a higher purpose. She had 146 tennis championships and was married to John Lloyd, but she said, "We get into a rut. We play tennis, we go to a movie, we watch TV, but I keep saying, 'John, there has to be more!'"

God has a higher purpose for His world than we often recognize. Most people see only a small part of the total picture of their lives, but God sees the end from the beginning. He is absolutely sovereign, which means He causes or allows all things to happen. The sovereignty of the Heavenly Father comforts His children in the most adverse circumstances.

Languishing under a huge sense of guilt for selling him into slavery, Joseph's brothers feared he would take revenge upon them once their father died. But Joseph was gracious and he had a greater view of God's sovereign plan. He wept over their mistrust and/or their genuine repentance and he forgave them completely. God had saved the world from starvation through his suffering. The dream of his brothers falling down before him was again fulfilled!

Joseph consistently gave all credit to God for everything good that happened. The God who brings good out of evil fulfilled His purposes for His people. When Joseph died at the age of 110 (a much younger age than Abraham, Isaac, or Jacob), he was embalmed and put in an Egyptian coffin. As a national hero, he was given a burial reserved for those of rank and wealth. But Joseph never forgot God's eternal promise to bring His people back to Canaan and to give them the land. He made his brothers swear to take his body with them when they returned! Sure enough, when God delivered Israel through Moses (400 years later), they took his bones along!

The book of Genesis closes with both death and hope. Mankind had fallen into sin and the resulting death shortly after creation. God had promised to send a Deliverer to "crush the serpent's head." Sin had progressively become worse, until finally God destroyed all but eight humans in the great flood. Then He selected a line of descendants to bring the Savior to earth. The nation of Israel was called by His sovereign will. Years later, the Deliverer would come to rule His people and His creation.

God sent a marvelous Deliverer! His name is Jesus Christ. Today He rules as Lord in the hearts of His people. Soon He will return to rule as King over His entire creation!

APPENDICES

Appendix I
Biblical Genealogy and Creation

God has given us enough information to closely (not exactly) determine the age of His creation. An accurate interpretation of scientific evidence confirms His Word. Genealogies in Genesis 5, 11, 21, and 25; Luke 3; and I Chronicles 1-8 are very helpful. Moses, under divine inspiration, wrote the book of Genesis. Several individuals, such as Adam (Genesis 1:1-5:1a), Noah (5:1b-6:9a), Shem (6:9b-11:10a), Terah (11:10b-11:27a), Isaac (11:27b-25:19a), Jacob (25:19b-37:2a), and Joseph (37:2b-50:21) could have passed written records down to him. Note the following chart from Adam to Jacob:

GENESIS 5

Patriarch	Year of Birth (since creation)	Age at Birth of Next Patriarch	Year of Death (since creation)
Adam	1	130	930
Seth	130	105	1042
Enos	235	90	1140
Cainan	325	70	1235
Mahalaleel	395	65	1290
Zared	460	162	1422
Enoch	622	65	(translated) 987
Methuselah	687	187	(flood) 1656
Lamech	874	182	1651
Noah	1056	500	2006
Shem	1558	100	2157

GENESIS 11

Arphaxad	1657	35	2097
Salah	1692	30	2125
Eber	1722	34	2186
Peleg (Babel)	1756	30	1995
Reu	1786	32	2025
Serug	1818	30	2048
Nahor	1848	29	1996
Terah	1877	70	2082
Abraham	1947	100	2122

GENESIS 21, 25 AND 47

Isaac	2047	60	2227
Jacob	2107	91	2254

Jacob was 130 when he moved to Egypt (Genesis 47:9). This was approximately 2,237 years since creation. Israel was in Egypt for 430 years (Exodus 12:40), so the Exodus from Egypt began 2,667 years from creation. From the exodus until Solomon began building the temple was 480 years (I Kings 6:1), 3,147 years since creation. The temple was built in the fourth year of Solomon's reign and he reigned a total of 40 years (I Kings 11:42), or until 3,183 years after creation. After Solomon's reign, Israel was split into two kingdoms. From historical records, we know that occurred in 931 B.C.! Adding 931 to 3,153 gives us approximately 4,114 years from creation until Jesus came! We must say "approximately" for several reasons. First, we know only the year, not the day of birth, of succeeding sons in the genealogies. Nor are we given the exact day of some recorded events. Second, during the reign of the kings of Israel (931 to 586 B.C.), a succeeding son sometimes began to reign during the lifetime of his father and there may be overlap. Third, it is uncertain whether or not to count the year a king began to reign as his first year. Fourth, the sacred year began with Nisan (first month) and the civil year began with Tishri (seventh month). We don't know which was used. Nevertheless, it's possible to be very close in dating the age of creation by studying and believing the Word of God! Jesus came to earth 2,000 years ago. Therefore, the Bible indicates that the creation is approximately 6,100 years old.

Appendix II

The Winning Run

PERHAPS YOU HAVE READ this book but never personally trusted the Savior with your earthly life and your
eternal destiny. The following baseball illustration explains
how you can come to know the Lord Jesus Christ:

In baseball, a runner must touch all four bases to
score a run for his team. The path to abundant and eternal life is very similar to the base paths on a ball diamond.

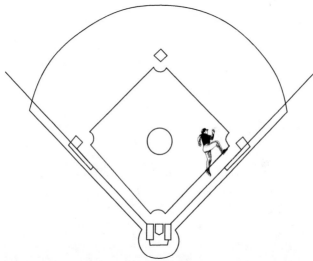

Step 1 (FIRST BASE) along that path is realizing that God
cares about you. He not only created you, but He also
loves you very deeply. He is seeking to give you an abundant life now and for eternity.

*For God so loved the world that He gave His one and only
Son, that whoever believes in Him shall not perish but
have eternal life.*

John 3:16

*I have come that they may have life, and have it to the
full.*

John 10:10

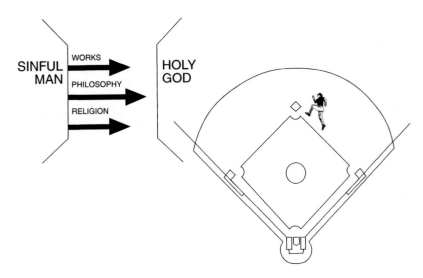

At SECOND BASE (step 2), we admit that we are sinners and separated from God. He is perfect, pure, and good; we are not. Because by nature we disobey Him and resist Him, He cannot have fellowship with us without denying His goodness and holiness. Instead, He must judge us.

Whoever believes in Him is not condemned; but whoever does not believe stands condemned already, because he has not believed in the name of God's one and only Son.
John 3:18

We realize we can never reach God through our own efforts. They do not solve the problem of our sin.

For all have sinned and come short of the glory of God.
Romans 3:23

But your iniquities have separated you from your God; your sins have hidden His face from you, so that He will not hear.
Isaiah 59:2

For the wages of sin is death, but the gift of God is eternal life in Christ Jesus our Lord.
Romans 6:23

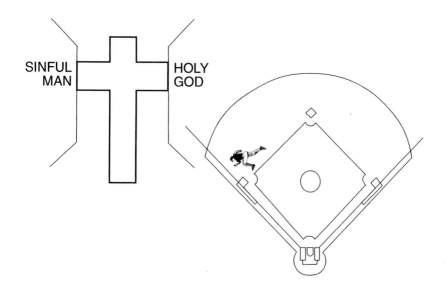

Third base is so close to scoring. Here (step 3) we understand that God has sent His Son, Jesus Christ, to die on the cross in payment for our sins. By His sacrifice, we may advance Home.

But God demonstrates His own love for us in this: While we were still sinners, Christ died for us.

Romans 5:8

For Christ died for sins once for all, the righteous for the unrighteous, to bring you to God.

I Peter 3:18

Jesus answered, "I am the way and the truth and the life. No one comes to the Father except through Me."

John 14:6

However, being CLOSE to Home does NOT count!

The Winning Run!

To score (step 4), we must personally receive Jesus Christ as Savior and Lord of our lives. We must not only realize that He died to rescue people from their sin but we must also trust Him to rescue us from our own sin. We cannot "squeeze" ourselves home any other way, and He will not force Himself upon us.

Yet to all who received Him, to those who believed in His name, He gave the right to become children of God.

John 1:12

For it is by grace you have been saved, through faith — and this is not from yourselves, it is the gift of God — not by works, so that no one can boast.

Ephesians 2:8-9

Why not receive Jesus Christ as your Savior and Lord right now? Simply say: "Yes, Lord," to His offer to forgive you for your sins and to change you.

_____
(signed)

_____
(date)

Tell someone of your decision and keep studying God's Word. These things greatly strengthen you (Romans 10:9-10). You may write CROSS TRAINING PUBLISHING for further encouragement. We would be thrilled to hear of your commitment! Welcome to eternal life!

CROSS TRAINING PUBLISHING
P.O. Box 1541
Grand Island, NE 68802

154

Appendix III

The Perfect Reliever

THE FOLLOWING BASEBALL illustration explains how to walk consistently in the power of the Holy Spirit, our only hope for victory in spiritual warfare.

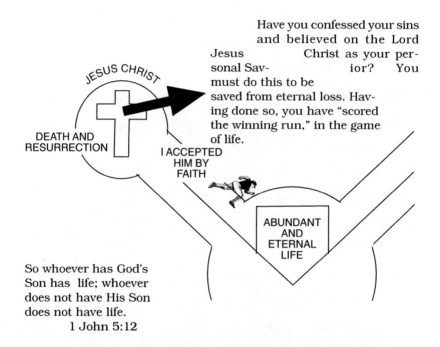

Have you confessed your sins and believed on the Lord Jesus Christ as your personal Savior? You must do this to be saved from eternal loss. Having done so, you have "scored the winning run," in the game of life.

JESUS CHRIST

DEATH AND RESURRECTION

I ACCEPTED HIM BY FAITH

ABUNDANT AND ETERNAL LIFE

So whoever has God's Son has life; whoever does not have His Son does not have life.
1 John 5:12

YOU SIGNED WITH THE WINNING TEAM WHEN YOU RECEIVED CHRIST!

1. Your sins were forgiven (Colossians 1:14).
2. You became a child of God (John 1:12).
3. God in dwelt you with His Spirit so you may live victoriously over the world (John 15:18-19), the flesh (Romans 7:15-18), and the devil (1 Peter 5:8).
4. You began the process of discovering God's purpose for your life (Romans 8:29).

BUT. . . .WHAT'S HAPPENING NOW?

Though our Lord has assured all His children of eternal life (John 10:28) and our position in Christ never changes, our practice may sometimes bring dishonor to God. The enemy rally makes life miserable.

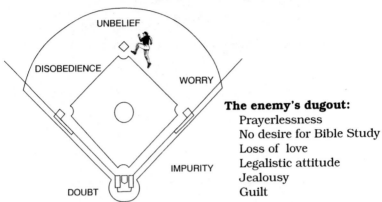

The enemy's dugout:
Prayerlessness
No desire for Bible Study
Loss of love
Legalistic attitude
Jealousy
Guilt

This rally must be stopped, for the Bible makes it clear that no one who belongs to God can continually practice sin (I John 2:3; 3:6-10).

These two pitchers' mounds represent the two lifestyles from which a Christian must choose:

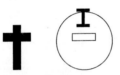

Self in control of the game and Christ's Resurrection power waiting in the bullpen — enemy rally produces discord.

For we naturally love to do evil things that are just the opposite from the things that the Holy Spirit tells us to do;

Power of Christ replaces self on the mound — rally is stopped and peace is restored.

. . . and the good things we want to do when the Spirit has His way with us are just the opposite of our natural desires.
Galatians 5:17a

SO, WHAT'S THE SOLUTION?

156

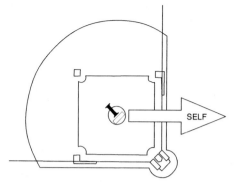

BRING IN THE PERFECT RELIEVER!

We must step off the mound and allow God to have complete authority by giving control of the game to the Holy Spirit.

Only by giving the Holy Spirit of God His rightful place of authority over our every thought, word and deed, can we consistently overcome defeat and despair.

If we are living now by the Holy Spirit's power, let us follow the Holy Spirit's leading in every part of our lives (Galatians 5:25).

WHAT DOES THE HOLY SPIRIT DO?

When you received Jesus Christ as Savior, the Holy Spirit *indwelt* you (Romans 8:9). Though all who have received Christ are indwelt by the Spirit, not all are *filled* (empowered, motivated) by the Spirit.

The Holy Spirit:
  a. Instructs us in all things (John 14:25-27).
  b. Always glorifies Jesus Christ (John 15:26; 16:13-15).
  c. Convicts us when things are wrong in our lives. (John 16:7-8).
  d. Helps us to share Christ with others (Acts 1:8).
  e. Assures us we belong to Christ (Romans 8:26).
  f. Enables us to live above circumstances through prayer (Romans 8:26).
  g. Flows from us as the source of an abundant and victorious life. (John 7:37-39).

HOW CAN YOU BE FILLED?

You can be filled (motivated) by the Holy Spirit right now IF YOU ARE WILLING to step off the mound of your life and give the ball to the Master Coach.

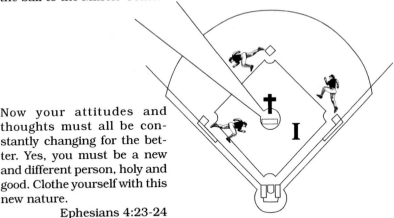

Now your attitudes and thoughts must all be constantly changing for the better. Yes, you must be a new and different person, holy and good. Clothe yourself with this new nature.
Ephesians 4:23-24

The Master Coach will not replace you on the mound against your heart's desire. Just as in receiving Christ, living consistently in His power is a matter of your will.

The Keys to Victory: Romans 6 (NAS)

A. KNOWING THIS, that our old self was crucified with Him that our body of sin might be done away with, that we should no longer be slaves to sin; for he who has died is freed from sin! (vs. 6-7)

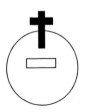

B. Even so, CONSIDER YOURSELVES TO BE DEAD to sin, but alive to God in Christ Jesus. (v. 11)

C. But PRESENT YOURSELVES TO GOD as those alive from the dead, and your members as instruments of righteousness to God. (v. 13b)

PRESENT YOURSELF TO GOD
THROUGH PRAYER

HERE IS A SUGGESTED PRAYER:

Dear Father,
I confess that I have taken control of my life and therefore have sinned against You. Thank You for forgiving me. I now CONSIDER myself dead to sin and PRESENT this body to You as a living sacrifice. I desire to be filled with Your Spirit as I live in obedience to Your WORD. Thank You for taking control of my life by the power of Your Spirit.

Amen.

HOW DO YOU KNOW YOU ARE FILLED BY THE HOLY SPIRIT?

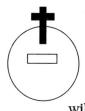 And we are sure of this, that He WILL listen to us whenever we ask Him for ANYTHING IN LINE WITH HIS WILL. And if we really KNOW He is listening when we talk to Him and make our requests, then we CAN BE SURE that He will answer us. 1 John 5:14-15

Is it God's will that you be filled (motivated) by His Spirit? He has said so (Ephesians 5:18). Therefore, based upon the authority of God's Word and His trustworthiness, you can KNOW you are filled with His Spirit regardless of your emotions.

WHAT WILL GOD'S PERFECT RELIEVER ACCOMPLISH IN YOUR LIFE?

He will retire all doubt, fear, worry and other sins that run the bases of your life. He will substitute love, joy, peace and other fruits (Galatians 5:22-23). His assortment of pitches includes truth, faith, righteousness and other weapons through which daily victory is assured (Ephesians 6:10-18). He will turn your eyes to the Master Coach, Jesus Christ, and conform you to His likeness (II Corinthians 3:18). You can praise and thank God through trials and suffering in the game of life, knowing He has a plan for you (James 1:2-4). The final score will bring much glory to God!

WHAT IF SELF TRIES TO GET BACK INTO THE GAME?

The self life is a deadly enemy of the control of the Holy Spirit. Often self will try to return to the game, and when that happens, Satan quickly reloads the bases. If you sense this happening, take these steps:

1) Confess all known sin to God and thank Him. He has forgiven you (1 John 1:9).

2) Trust Christ to again fill you with the Holy Spirit, Who will once more take control (Ephesians 5:18).

PLAYING THE GAME OF LIFE under His control will become a way of life, and you will experience constant victory! If "The Perfect Reliever" has been of help to you, please share it with a friend who also knows Jesus Christ as his personal Savior. He, too, can enjoy walking daily in the power of the Holy Spirit. May God bless you.

Elliot Johnson

For further information, please write:

Cross Training Publishing
P.O. Box 1541
Grand Island, NE 68802